# HANDS-ON
## COMPUTER ACTIVITIES
## for TEACHING MATH

# HANDS-ON
## COMPUTER ACTIVITIES
## for TEACHING MATH

### GRADES 3–8

◆

## BEVERLY BURNLEY

JOSSEY-BASS
A Wiley Imprint
www.josseybass.com

Published by Jossey-Bass
A Wiley Imprint
989 Market Street, San Francisco, CA 94103-1741  www.josseybass.com

Design and production by Navta Associates, Inc.

Jossey-Bass books and products are available through most bookstores. To contact Jossey-Bass
directly call our Customer Care Department within the U.S. at 800-956-7739, outside the U.S. at
317-572-3986 or fax 317-572-4002.

Jossey-Bass also publishes its books in a variety of electronic formats. Some content that appears
in print may not be available in electronic books.

*Library of Congress Cataloging-in-Publication Data*

Burnley, Beverly, date.
  Hands-on computer activities for teaching math : grades 3–8 / Beverly Burnley.—1st ed.
      p. cm.
  ISBN 0-471-65198-2 (paper : alk. paper)
  1. Mathematics—Study and teaching (Elementary)—Activity programs.
2. Computer-assisted instruction.  I. Title.
  QA135.6.B7684 2005
  372.7′044—dc22

                                                          2004014945

Printed in the United States of America
10  9  8  7  6  5  4  3  2  1

This book of computer activities is dedicated to

- the students at Donald McHenry Elementary School in East St. Louis, Illinois, who so enthusiastically performed the activities, and the faculty and staff who supported the activities.

- Gloria Oggero of the St. Clair County Regional Office of Education in Illinois who gave me the first opportunity to present the strategy to teachers.

- Brenda May, a retired supervisor for East St. Louis School District, who copresented the workshops.

- my mother and sisters.

- Rolanda, Donna, and Craig—my adult children who gave me my first computer.

# CONTENTS

· · · · · · · · · · · · · · · · · · · ·

**SECTION 3**

# MEASUREMENT,   89

## SECTION 4

# ALGEBRA,     125

## SECTION 5

# GEOMETRY,     165

**SECTION 6**

# DATA ANALYSIS AND PROBABILITY, 215

# ABOUT THIS BOOK

*Hands-On Computer Activities for Teaching Math* has been written to help teachers support the math standards using the software already on most computers, including Microsoft Word, Microsoft Excel, and Microsoft Paint or any other drawing program. Computer software can make abstract ideas become physical in the same way as math manipulatives.

Classroom math teachers and math specialists in grades 3 through 8 may use the simple instructions that accompany the activities as a guide for teaching the standards. The concepts may be adjusted to the desired level, and once the stage is set, the teacher should expand and develop the lesson.

The computer activities in this resource provide focus for class discussion about the models and images on the screen. After a guided lesson, students can be expected to create other models and explain concepts on their own. These independent activities will aid in assessment, allowing you to examine the processes and interpretations used by the student. The images may be printed for students to take home and explain to their parents, or displayed in the classroom as a reference.

For easy use, materials are organized into six sections and printed in a format that lies flat so that you can photocopy any activity as many times as needed. Section 1, "Getting Started," provides three activities for getting started with the Paint Tool Box. Sections 2 through 6 present 102 activities in five basic areas of math: Number and Operations, Measurement, Algebra, Geometry, and Data Analysis and Probability.

Each activity includes a descriptive title keyed to the math concept, a specific learning objective, step-by-step directions, and an illustration of the model. The directions are written in simple, nontechnical language and can be followed by students working on their own or in pairs once you have presented the activity in class.

These activities allow you to integrate computers into your math curriculum without waiting for on-site licenses. They will help your students learn math concepts and computer skills at the same time.

# ABOUT THE AUTHOR

Beverly Burnley earned her bachelor's degree in elementary education from Harris Stowe Teachers College in St. Louis, Missouri. As a Title I teacher in the East St. Louis (Illinois) public schools, she has used models and representations to teach mathematics to gifted and remedial students in grades 1 through 6 for more than thirty-three years. While instructing entire classrooms in a computer lab environment, she created a unique teaching strategy that supports the math standards and increases students' computer proficiency levels.

Ms. Burnley has presented this strategy for professional development workshops at the St. Clair County (Illinois) Regional Office of Education and now describes it for teachers across the country in her new book, *Hands-On Computer Activities for Teaching Math*.

# TEACHER TO TEACHER

. . . . . . . . . . . . . . . . . . . . . . . . . . . . . . . . . . . . . .

Elementary students enjoy using the computer. They also take great pride in things they create. The activities in this book capitalize on both students' enjoyment of using computers and students' creativity to teach many of the national math standards.

You will find that your students learn to use the toolbars very quickly. This is their generation of technology. Do not fear that the activities are too difficult. They are really very simple.

Ideally, these activities should be done in a computer lab. This setting allows the teacher to incorporate the National Council of Teachers of Mathematics (NCTM) Process Standards: connections, communication, representation, problem solving, and reasoning and proof. They may also be used as demonstration lessons for later individual work activities.

This resource serves as a tool for teachers of grades 3 through 8 to integrate computers into their math curriculum using the Microsoft software that is already on their computers. The activities allow for a constructivist teaching design. Most can be adapted to different grade levels.

Having taught lower- and upper-level elementary mathematics for over thirty-three years, I truly believe students learn math best by doing (especially by creating math images and modeling math concepts). Students will enjoy the colorful images and will become more proficient in using the computer.

# Section 1

# GETTING STARTED

# Getting Started with the Paint Tool Box

◆ ·  ·  ·  ·  ·  ·  ·  ·  ·  ·  ·  ·  ·  ·  ·  ◆  ·  ·  ·  ·  ·  ·  ·  ·  ·  ·  ·  ·  ·  ·  ·

The Microsoft Paint Tool Box is reproduced below along with an explanation of each tool's function. To change colors, use the Color Box at the bottom of the Paint screen.

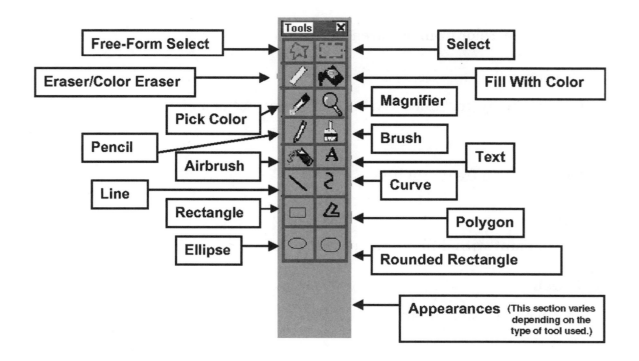

## Free-Form Select

- To select a free-form area by dragging the pointer around the area

## Select

- To copy and paste part of an image
- To erase (delete)
- To flip and rotate an image

*(continued)*

- To stretch or skew an image

**Eraser/Color Eraser**

- To erase a small area in white or in color

**Fill With Color**

- To color an enclosed area

**Pick Color**

- To copy color from one area to another

**Magnifier**

- To display grid lines and to zoom in and out of a picture

**Pencil**

- To draw a free-form line

**Brush**

- To paint with different-shaped brushes

**Airbrush**

- To paint using an airbrush effect

**Text**

- To type and format text

**Line**

- To draw straight and free-form lines

**Curve**

- To draw one or two arcs

**Rectangle**

*(continued)*

- To draw a rectangle or a square

## Polygon

- To draw polygons

## Ellipse

- To draw an ellipse or a circle

## Rounded Rectangle

- To draw a round-cornered rectangle or square

# The Starting Line

*Objective:* To represent different lines using the Line button in the Paint Tool Box

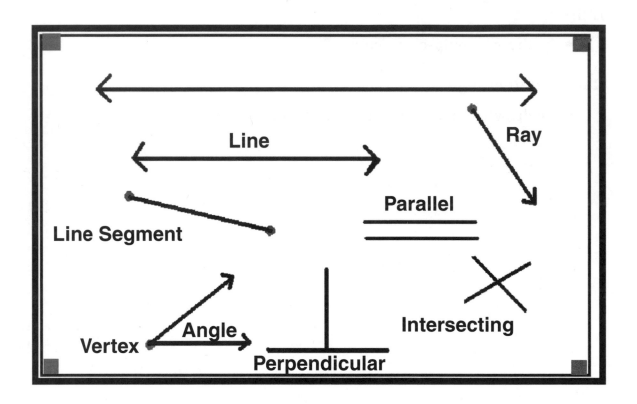

- A *line* is made up of points and is straight. It continues in opposite directions without ending. To show this, we draw an arrow on each end.

- A *line segment* or segment is the part of a line between two points. It is straight and has a beginning and an end. To show this, we may draw dots at each end or we may not.

- A *ray* is part of a line that has a beginning but no end. To show this, we draw a dot at one end and an arrow at the other end.

- *Parallel lines* are always the same distance apart and they never intersect.

*(continued)*

- *Perpendicular lines* cross or meet at right (90-degree) angles.

- *Intersecting lines* cross at a point.

- An *angle* is formed when two rays meet at a point. This point is called the *vertex*. The rays are called the sides of the angle.

1. Click on the Line button in the Tool Box and choose the thickest size from the section at the bottom of the Tool Box.

2. Click somewhere on the page, and while holding down the Shift key, drag a straight line across the page. (*Note:* Holding down the Shift key while dragging makes a straight line that will move in 45-degree angles. If you are using the Rectangle button, holding down the Shift key will make a perfect square, and if you are using the Ellipse button, holding down the Shift key will make a perfect circle.) Release the mouse first, then release the Shift key to end the line.

3. Use the method in step 2 to draw arrows at the ends of the line. You have drawn the symbol for a line.

4. In the Color Box, right click on red and left click on red. (This will make the foreground and the background of the shape you draw red.)

5. Click on the Ellipse button in the Tool Box and choose the opaque symbol at the bottom of the Tool Box (shaded box with an outline). Click on a spot on the page and make a small red dot by holding the left mouse button down and dragging the mouse slightly.

6. Click on the Select button in the Tool Box and choose the transparent symbol at the bottom of the Tool Box. Select the red dot on the page by clicking and dragging over the area with the mouse.

7. Go to Edit and choose Copy.

8. Go to Edit and choose Paste.

9. Hold the left button on the mouse down and move the pasted dot to a spot away from the original dot.

10. Choose the Line button and the color black from the Color Box (right click on white and left click on black). Drag a line connecting the two dots.

*(continued)*

**11.** Drag another line on the page without the dots at the ends. You have drawn the symbols for a line segment or segment.

**12.** Go to Edit and choose Paste.

**13.** Drag the pasted dot to a position on the screen.

**14.** Click on the Line button and drag a line from the dot. Draw an arrow at the end of the line. You have drawn the symbol for a ray.

**15.** Go to Edit and choose Paste.

**16.** Use the left mouse button to drag the pasted dot to a position on the screen.

**17.** Click on the Line button and draw two rays extending from the dot in different directions. You have drawn an angle with two sides.

**18.** To label your drawings, click on the Text button and click and drag an area on the page to make a text box. Choose Arial font, size 14, and type a label in the text box. Label the following: line, line segment, ray, vertex, and side.

**19.** To move your labels to the right spots, click on the Select button, outline the words, and move them next to their symbols.

**20.** Looking at your symbols, compare a line to a line segment, compare a line to a ray, and compare a ray to a line segment.

**21.** Click on the Text button, create a text box, and type your observations.

**22.** Practice using the Line button to draw the parallel, perpendicular, and intersecting lines, as shown in the art at the beginning of this activity.

# Line Design

· · · · · · · · · · · · · · · · · · ◆ · · · · · · · · · · · · · · · · · ·

*Objective:* To practice using the Line and Fill With Color buttons in the Paint Tool Box and to recognize shapes as an art form

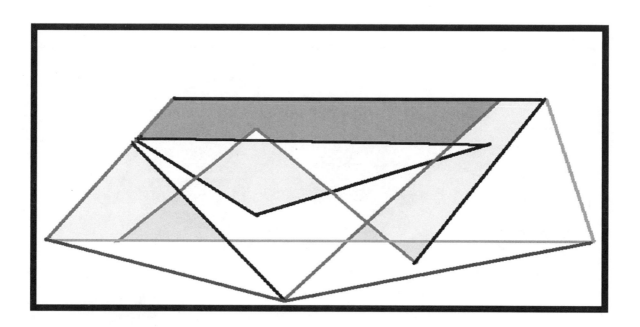

1. Click on the Line button and choose the size of the line at the bottom of the Tool Box. Click on any color in the Color Box and drag a line on the page. (To drag a line, hold down the left button on the mouse and let go when you want the line to end.)

2. Create a line design by dragging different sizes and colors of lines in different directions.

3. You may choose the Fill With Color button to highlight your design. When using this button, remember that the area being colored must be completely closed.

4. Discuss some of the properties of your design. (What shapes do you see?)

# The Bouncing Ball

· · · · · · · · · · · · · · ◆ · · · · · · · · · · · · · ·

*Objective:* To learn to use the Select button and the Ellipse button in the Paint Tool Box, and the foreground and background options of the Paint Color Box

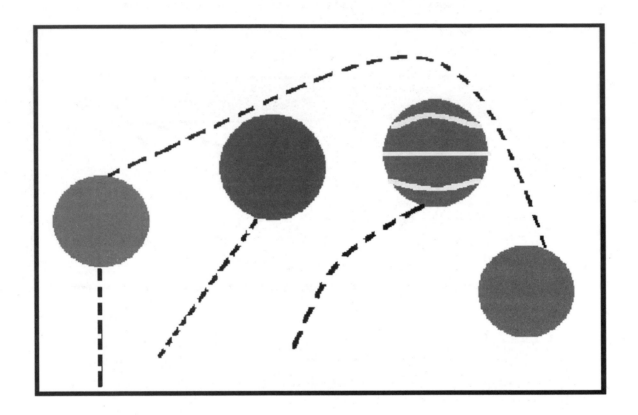

● A *circle* is the set of all points in a plane at a fixed distance, called the *radius*, from a fixed point, called the *center*.

1. Left click on red, then right click on red in the Color Box.

2. Click on the Ellipse button and choose the opaque symbol from the section at the bottom of the Tool Box.

3. While holding down the Shift key, drag a red circle on the screen. Release the mouse, then release the Shift key. (This creates a perfect circle.)

*(continued)*

4. Left click on blue and right click on white in the Color Box.

5. Choose the transparent symbol from the section at the bottom of the Tool Box. While holding down the Shift key, click and drag a circle with a blue outline.

6. Click on the Fill With Color button and click inside the circle to color it blue.

7. Click on the Select button and choose the transparent symbol at the bottom of the Tool Box. Use the left mouse button to drag a box around the red circle. (The Select button is used to copy and paste and to move images or text.)

8. Go to Edit and choose Copy.

9. Go to Edit and choose Paste.

10. Click on the pasted circle and hold down the left button on the mouse to move the pasted circle anywhere on the page. Release the mouse button when the circle is where you want it.

11. Left click outside the box.

12. Click on the Fill With Color button, choose green from the Color Box, and click on the pasted circle to color it green.

13. Color any of the other balls as you wish.

14. Click on the Select button and choose the transparent symbol at the bottom of the Tool Box. Click on any of the circles and bounce them on the screen like a ball.

# Section 2

NUMBER AND
OPERATIONS

# Addition and Subtraction Facts

◆

*Objective:* To identify and model the relationship between addition and subtraction and the commutative property of addition using the Paint Tool Box and Color Box

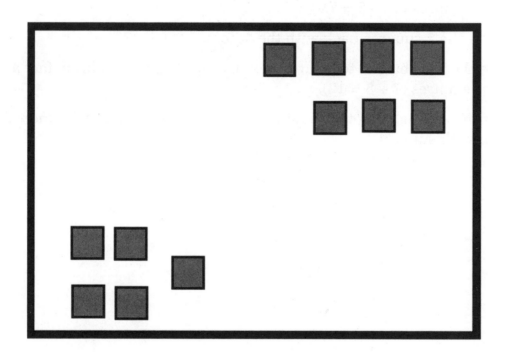

1. Click on the Rectangle button and choose transparent from the section at the bottom of the Tool Box.

2. Hold down the Shift key and the left mouse button. Drag a small square. Release the mouse, then release the shift key. (This will make a perfect square.)

3. Click on the Fill With Color button and choose a color from the Color Box. Color the square.

4. Click on the Select button and choose the transparent option at the bottom of the Tool Box. Drag a box around the square.

*(continued)*

5. Go to Edit and choose Copy.

6. Go to Edit and choose Paste. Move the square next to the first square.

7. Continue to paste until you have a total of 12 squares.

8. Click on the Select button and drag a box around a set of 5 squares.

9. Move the selected set away from the others. How many squares are left?

10. Use the Text button to create a text box and type a subtraction fact about your squares ($12 - 5 = 7$).

11. Move the 5 squares back with the others.

12. Use the Text button to create a text box and type an addition fact about your squares ($7 + 5 = 12$).

13. Continue to select sets of squares and type facts for addition and subtraction with sums of 12.

# Constructing an Addition Table

························◆·····················

*Objective:* To develop an understanding of the effects of addition and to become proficient with basic addition facts using the Tables and Borders toolbar in Microsoft Word

| + | 0 | 1 | 2 | 3 | 4 | 5 | 6 | 7 | 8 | 9 |
|---|---|---|---|---|---|---|---|---|---|---|
| 0 | 0 | 1 | 2 | 3 | 4 | 5 | 6 | 7 | 8 | 9 |
| 1 | 1 | 2 | 3 | 4 | 5 | 6 | 7 | 8 | 9 | 10 |
| 2 | 2 | 3 | 4 | 5 | 6 | 7 | 8 | 9 | 10 | 11 |
| 3 | 3 | 4 | 5 | 6 | 7 | 8 | 9 | 10 | 11 | 12 |
| 4 | 4 | 5 | 6 | 7 | 8 | 9 | 10 | 11 | 12 | 13 |
| 5 | 5 | 6 | 7 | 8 | 9 | 10 | 11 | 12 | 13 | 14 |
| 6 | 6 | 7 | 8 | 9 | 10 | 11 | 12 | 13 | 14 | 15 |
| 7 | 7 | 8 | 9 | 10 | 11 | 12 | 13 | 14 | 15 | 16 |
| 8 | 8 | 9 | 10 | 11 | 12 | 13 | 14 | 15 | 16 | 17 |
| 9 | 9 | 10 | 11 | 12 | 13 | 14 | 15 | 16 | 17 | 18 |

1. In Microsoft Word, go to View Toolbars, and choose the Tables and Borders toolbar.

2. Click on the Insert Table button.

3. In the message box, type 11 for the number of columns and 11 for the number of rows.

4. Choose OK.

5. Select the inserted table by clicking in the first cell and dragging the mouse until the entire table is selected.

*(continued)*

**6.** On the Formatting toolbar, select Arial Black font, size 22, center align, and black color.

**7.** Left click outside the table.

**8.** Place the pointer on the outside of the first row and left click to select that row.

**9.** Choose the color red on the Formatting toolbar.

**10.** Click in the first cell and type the plus sign. Type the numbers 0 through 9 in the following cells on that row. (You may use the Tab key, the Right Arrow key, or the mouse to move to the next cell.)

**11.** Place the pointer on the outside of the first column until a black arrow appears and left click to select the first column.

**12.** Choose the color red on the Formatting toolbar.

**13.** Starting in the second row and going down the first column, type the numbers 0 through 9. You may use the Down Arrow key or the mouse to move down the column.

**14.** Select the first cell and change the + sign to blue.

**15.** Fill in each cell by adding the red number at the top of the column and the red number at the left of the row for that cell. This is the sum.

**16.** Click and drag over each of the odd sums in the table to select them, then choose the Highlight button on the Formatting toolbar to highlight all the odd sums in yellow.

**17.** Describe a pattern you notice in your table. Make and record a conclusion about odd sums (Even + Odd = Odd).

**18.** Make and record a conclusion about even sums (Even + Even = Even, and Odd + Odd = Even).

**19.** The commutative property of addition states that it does not matter in which order the elements are combined. Use your table to demonstrate the commutative property of addition.

**20.** You may print the addition table and use it to practice your addition facts.

# Addition and Subtraction on a Number Line

◆

*Objectives:* To identify and model the relationship between addition and subtraction using the Paint Tool Box and Color Box; to identify and model the commutative property of addition using the Paint Tool Box and Color Box

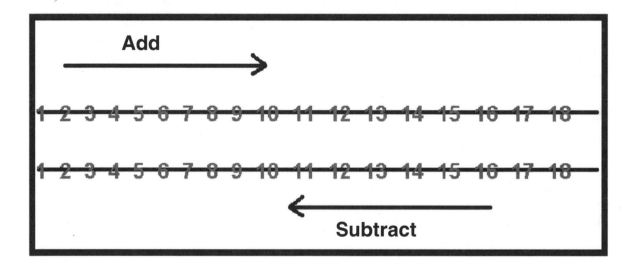

1. Click on the Line button and use the mouse to drag (while holding down the Shift key) a straight line all the way across the screen.

2. Click on the Text button and select the first option from the section at the bottom of the Tool Box. Use the mouse to click and drag a text box around the line so that the line is centered in the box.

3. Go to View and choose Text Toolbar.

4. On the Text Toolbar, choose Arial font, size 20.

5. Choose red in the Color Box.

6. Type the numbers 1 through 18 on the line with a space between each number. This is a number line to use for addition and subtraction.

*(continued)*

**7.** When adding on the number line, move to the right.

**8.** To add 9 plus 6, place your finger on 9 and add (count to the right) 6 steps.

**9.** What number is 6 more than 9? (Where did you stop?)

**10.** The numbers 6 and 9 are addends for the sum 15. Therefore, 9 + 6 = 15.

**11.** To add 6 plus 9, place your finger on 6 and count to the right 9 steps.

**12.** What number is 9 more than 6? (15). Therefore, 6 + 9 = 15.

**13.** Showing that 9 + 6 = 15 and 6 + 9 = 15 is an example of the commutative property of addition.

**14.** Try adding 8 + 5 and 5 + 8 on the number line.

**15.** What number did you stop on both times? (13).

**16.** How does this show the commutative property of addition?

**17.** When subtracting on the number line, move to the left.

**18.** Use the number line to work out the following problem: Mary had 17 pencils. She gave 8 to her friends. How many did she have left?

**19.** This is a subtraction problem; Mary is giving away some of her pencils.

**20.** To subtract 17 minus 8, place your finger on 17 and count 8 steps to the left.

**21.** What number is 8 less than 17? (9). Therefore, 17 − 8 = 9.

**22.** To subtract 17 minus 9, place your finger on 17 and count 9 steps to the left.

**23.** What number is 9 less than 17? (8). Therefore, 17 − 9 = 8.

**24.** Work with a partner to explore other addition and subtraction facts (9 + 5, 4 + 8, 8 + 7, 12 − 4, 14 − 5, 15 − 7, and so on).

# Place Value Table

*Objective:* To represent base-ten numbers using the Microsoft Word Tables and Borders and Drawing toolbars

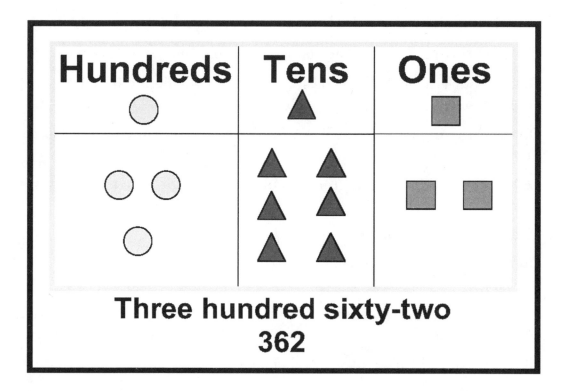

1. In Microsoft Word, go to View, and select the Tables and Borders toolbar.

2. On the Tables and Borders toolbar, click on Insert Table.

3. In the message box, type 3 for columns and 2 for rows. Click on OK.

4. Left click the mouse to the left of the first cell to highlight the first row.

5. On the Formatting toolbar, choose Center align, Arial font, size 36, bold, and black color.

6. Click outside the table.

7. Type "Hundreds" in the first cell and press Enter.

*(continued)*

8. Use the Tab key to move to the middle cell and type "Tens."

9. Use the Tab key to move to the next cell and type "Ones."

10. Go to View and choose the Drawing toolbar.

11. On the Drawing toolbar, choose AutoShapes, Basic Shapes, and Oval.

12. Left click under the word "Hundreds" to insert a circle.

13. On the Drawing Toolbar, click on the Fill Color button and choose yellow.

14. To size your circle, click on the shape and use the field handles to stretch or shorten it.

15. On the Drawing toolbar, choose AutoShapes, Basic Shapes, and Isosceles Triangle.

16. Left click under the word "Tens" to insert a triangle. Move and size your triangle as needed.

17. Click on the Fill Color button and choose red.

18. On the Drawing toolbar, choose Auto Shapes, Basic Shapes, and Rectangle.

19. Left click under the word "Ones" to insert a square. Move and size your square as needed.

20. Click on the Fill Color button and choose green.

21. To model the number 362, click on each shape and go to Edit to copy and paste the number of shapes for each place value in the second row. You will have to move each shape into position in the correct cell after pasting. To increase the sizes of the cells, press Enter.

22. Work with a partner to model other numbers. (You may wish to change shapes and colors.)

# Modeling Whole Numbers

◆

*Objective:* To develop an understanding of the base-ten numbers in expanded notation using the Paint Tool Box and Color Box

Note: This activity may be done after using place value blocks.

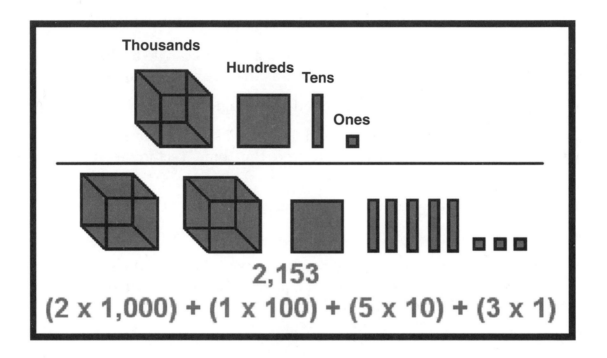

1. Click on the Rectangle button and choose transparent from the section at the bottom of the Tool Box. Click anywhere on the page and drag (while holding down the Shift key) a small square.

2. Click on the Select button and choose transparent from the section at the bottom of the Tool Box. Click and drag over the square to select it.

3. Go to Edit and choose Copy.

4. Go to Edit and choose Paste.

5. Move the pasted square by clicking and dragging until the upper left corner is in the center of the original square.

(continued)

6. Click on the Line button and drag four lines to connect the corners of the two squares to form a cube.

7. Click on the Text button and drag a text box to label the cube "Thousands."

8. Go to Edit and choose Paste. Move this new square to the right of the cube.

9. Drag a text box and label the square "Hundreds."

10. Click on the Rectangle button and drag a thin rectangle to the right of the "Hundreds" square that is as tall as the "Hundreds" square.

11. Click on the text button and label the rectangle "Tens."

12. Click on the Rectangle button and drag (while holding down the Shift key) a very small square to the right of the "Tens" rectangle (about one-tenth of the "Tens").

13. Click on the Text button and label the small square "Ones."

14. Drag another text box on the page and type a number (up to four digits).

15. Click on the Select button and choose transparent from the section at the bottom of the Tool Box. Click on the place value block needed to model the number to select that block.

16. Go to Edit and choose Copy.

17. Go to Edit and choose Paste.

18. Move the pasted block to the proper place in the model for the number that you typed.

19. Continue to copy and paste until you have modeled each place value.

20. Click on the Text button and type the number that you modeled in an expanded notation form.

21. Try giving numbers to a classmate to model.

# Color Tile Place Value

*Objective:* To develop an understanding of place value using the Paint Tool Box and Color Box

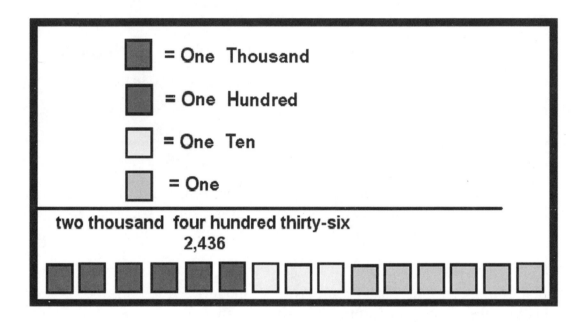

1. Click on the Rectangle button, then click on the screen and drag (while holding down the Shift key) a small square tile.

2. Click on the Select button and chose transparent from the section at the bottom of the Tool Box. Click and drag around the square to select it.

3. Go to Edit and choose Copy.

4. Go to Edit and choose Paste.

5. Move the pasted tile under the original tile.

6. Go to Edit and choose Paste to paste two more tiles and move them under the other two tiles in a column.

7. Click on the Fill With Color button and color the tiles from top to bottom red, blue, yellow, and green.

*(continued)*

8.  Click on the Text button and click and drag a text box next to the red tile.

9.  Go to View and choose Text Toolbar.

10. On the Text Toolbar, choose Arial font, size 16, and bold.

11. Type "= One Thousand" in the text box.

12. Click and drag a text box next to the blue tile and type "= One Hundred."

13. Click and drag a text box next to the yellow tile and type "= One Ten."

14. Click and drag a text box next to the green tile and type "= One."

15. Choose a four-digit number.

16. Click and drag a text box under the tile column and type the number both in words and in number form.

17. Click on the Select button and choose transparent from the section at the bottom of the Tool Box. To model your number, select the color tiles you need and copy and paste them below the number.

18. Exchange numbers with a classmate to model.

19. Model more numbers and compare your models. Which number is greatest? Explain how you can tell by using the model.

# Moving Places

◆

*Objective:* To develop an understanding of the base-ten place value system using the Paint Tool Box and Color Box

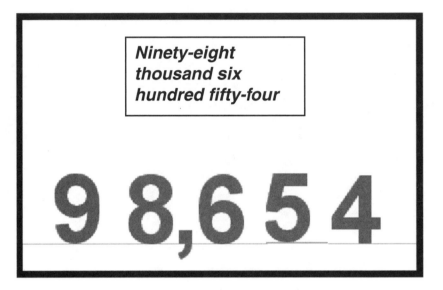

1. Click on the Text button.

2. Go to View and choose Text Toolbar. Choose Arial font, size 72, and red color.

3. Click and drag a text box on the page and type five one-digit numbers (given to you by your teacher) and a comma. Insert two spaces between the numbers.

4. Left click outside the text box.

5. Click on the Select button and choose transparent from the section at the bottom of the Tool Box.

6. Select the comma and move it near the bottom of the screen.

7. Select and move the five digits to make the lowest and highest numbers possible.

8. Click on the Text button and choose font size 24.

*(continued)*

9. Click and drag a text box above your numbers and type the numbers in words.

10. Type digits with a partner and move them to create the lowest and highest numbers.

11. Click and drag a text box in which you explain how you made the lowest and highest numbers. (Where did you place these numbers?)

# Ordinal Numbers

*Objective:* To identify and name the position held in a series using the Paint Tool Box and Color Box

First   Second   Third   Fourth   Fifth   Sixth   Seventh

- *Ordinal numbers* name the position held in a series.

1. Use the Ellipse and Line tools to draw a stick figure.

2. Click on the Select button and choose transparent from the section at the bottom of the Tool Box. Click on the stick figure to select it.

3. Go to Edit and choose Copy.

4. Go to Edit and choose Paste.

5. Move the pasted figure.

6. Continue to paste and move until there are seven figures in a row.

7. Click on the Line button and choose the color red from the Color Box. Draw a *red triangle dress* on one figure.

(continued)

8.  Click on the Ellipse button and click and drag a *yellow circle skirt* on one figure.

9.  Click on the Rectangle button and click and drag a *green square shirt* on one figure.

10. Click on the Line button and draw a *gray trapezoid skirt* on one figure.

11. Still using the Line button, change colors to draw a *brown bow tie* on one figure.

12. Click on the Rectangle button to draw an *orange rectangular hat* on one figure.

13. Still using the Rectangle button, change colors to draw a *blue rectangular shirt* on one figure.

14. Click on the Fill With Color button and fill in all the colors.

15. Click on the Select button and select and move the figures so that the third figure in line has a green square shirt, the fifth figure has an orange rectangular hat, the first figure has a blue rectangular shirt, the last figure has a gray trapezoid skirt, the figure with the yellow circle skirt is in front of the figure with the green square shirt, the figure with the red triangle dress is behind the figure with the green square shirt, and the figure with the brown bow tie is next to last in line.

16. Click on the Text button and click and drag a text box.

17. Go to View and choose Text Toolbar. Pick size 12 font and bold. Then type the words "First," "Second," "Third," "Fourth," "Fifth," "Sixth," and "Seventh."

18. Click on the Select button and click and drag the ordinal number words under the appropriate figures.

# Ordering Numbers

◆

*Objective:* To order and compare whole numbers using the Paint Tool Box and Color Box

| 6 8 3 5 | |
|---|---|
| 8,653 | 5,863 |
| 8,635 | 5,836 |
| 8,563 | 5,683 |
| 8,536 | 5,638 |
| 8,365 | 5,386 |
| 8,356 | 5,368 |
| 6,853 | 3,865 |
| 6,835 | 3,856 |
| 6,583 | 3,685 |
| 6,538 | 3,658 |
| 6,385 | 3,586 |
| 6,358 | 3,568 |

, , , , , , , , , ,
, , , , , , , , , ,
, , , , , , , , , ,

1. Click on the Text button and click and drag a text box. Type the numbers 6 8 3 5 (put three spaces between each number).

2. Create another text box and type three rows of commas.

3. Click on the Line button and choose black from the Color Box. Click and drag a straight line (while holding down the Shift key) under the numbers. You will use these numbers to construct four-digit numbers, ordering the numbers from the highest to the lowest. How many numbers do you think are possible? You will make an organized list to find the answer.

*(continued)*

**4.** Click on the Select button and select the row of numbers.

**5.** Go to Edit and choose Copy.

**6.** Go to Edit and choose Paste.

**7.** Rearrange the pasted numbers to construct the highest number. Since 8 is the highest number, it should be in the thousands place. Six should be in the hundreds place, 5 in the tens place, and 3 in the ones place.

**8.** Continue to paste and rearrange the numbers until you have ordered five more numbers that have 8 in the thousands place.

**9.** Continue to paste and order the numbers until you have constructed six numbers for each different number in the thousands place. How many total numbers are on the list? Is this the number you guessed?

**10.** Click on the Select button and click and drag the commas into position between the thousands and hundreds place.

**11.** Work with a partner to order and construct another set of numbers.

# Comparing Numbers on a Venn Diagram

*Objective:* To recognize and graph the comparison of numbers on a Venn diagram using the Paint Tool Box

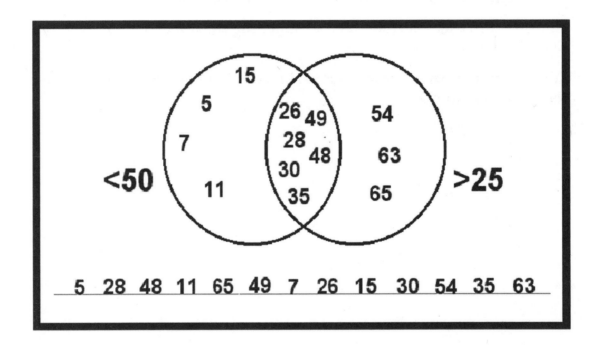

- A *Venn diagram* is a graph used to show sets. A region inside a circle represents the different sets.

1.  Click on the Text button and create a text box to type the numbers 5, 28, 48, 11, 65, 49, 7, 26, 15, 30, 54, 30, 54, 35, and 63.

2.  Click on the Ellipse button and click and drag (while holding down the Shift key) a circle on the page.

3.  Click on the Select button and choose transparent from the section at the bottom of the Tool Box. Click on the circle.

*(continued)*

**4.** Go to Edit and choose Copy.

**5.** Go to Edit and choose Paste.

**6.** Drag the pasted circle to make it overlap on the original. This will be the Venn diagram.

**7.** Click on the Text button and create text boxes outside the circles. Label one circle <50 and the other circle >25. The overlap section on the diagram is for numbers that have both characteristics (<50 and >25).

**8.** Click on the Select button and click and drag the numbers to their proper place in the diagram.

**9.** Work with a partner to construct and label a Venn diagram that shows different sets of numbers.

# Arrays and Fact Families

· · · · · · · · · · · · · · · · · · · · · · · · ◆ · · · · · · · · · · · · · · · · · · · · · · · ·

*Objective:* To identify and use relationships between multiplication and division using the Paint Tool Box and Color Box

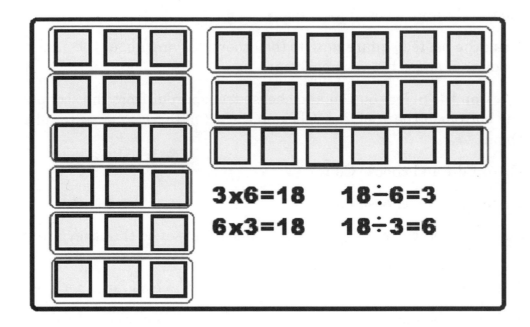

$$3 \times 6 = 18 \qquad 18 \div 6 = 3$$
$$6 \times 3 = 18 \qquad 18 \div 3 = 6$$

- An *array* is an arrangement of rows and columns, with each row having the same number of objects and each column having the same number of objects.

1. You will model the fact family for $3 \times 6 = 18$. Click on the Line button and choose the third thickest line from the section at the bottom of the Tool Box.

2. Click on the Rectangle button and click and drag (while holding down the Shift key) a square (about one-half inch on a side) on the page.

3. Click on the Fill With Color button and pick a color from the Color Box to color the square.

4. Click on the Select button and select the square.

*(continued)*

5. Go to Edit and choose Copy.

6. Go to Edit and choose Paste.

7. Drag the pasted square next to the original, leaving a little space between the two.

8. Go to Edit and choose Paste again.

9. Drag the pasted square next to the others, leaving about the same amount of space between each one.

10. Click on the Select button and choose transparent from the section at the bottom of the Tool Box. Click on the set of three squares to select them.

11. Go to Edit and choose Copy.

12. Go to Edit and choose Paste.

13. Drag the pasted set of squares below the first set so that they are evenly aligned.

14. Continue to paste until you have six rows of three squares per row.

15. How many squares are there? Three times six is eighteen ($3 \times 6 = 18$). You have created an array.

16. Click on the Select button and select the entire array.

17. Go to Edit and choose Copy.

18. Go to Edit and choose Paste.

19. Drag the pasted array apart from the other array.

20. While the new array is still selected, go to Image and choose Flip/Rotate.

21. Choose Rotate by angle 90° and click on OK. This array now has three rows of sets of six ($6 \times 3 = 18$), which shows that multiplication is commutative.

22. Click on the Rectangle button and frame six sets of three. Eighteen divided into six sets is three in each set ($18 \div 6 = 3$).

*(continued)*

**23.** Click on the Rectangle button and frame three even sets. How many are in each set? ($18 \div 3 = 6$)

**24.** Click on the Text button and click and drag a text box. In the box, type the fact family you demonstrated.

**25.** Work with a partner to model another fact family.

# Constructing a
# Multiplication Table

◆

*Objective:* To create a table of multiplication facts for practice and other activities using the Tables and Borders toolbar in Microsoft Word

| x | 1 | 2 | 3 | 4 | 5 | 6 | 7 | 8 | 9 | 10 |
|----|----|----|----|----|----|----|----|----|----|-----|
| 1 | 1 | 2 | 3 | 4 | 5 | 6 | 7 | 8 | 9 | 10 |
| 2 | 2 | 4 | 6 | 8 | 10 | 12 | 14 | 16 | 18 | 20 |
| 3 | 3 | 6 | 9 | 12 | 15 | 18 | 21 | 24 | 27 | 30 |
| 4 | 4 | 8 | 12 | 16 | 20 | 24 | 28 | 32 | 36 | 40 |
| 5 | 5 | 10 | 15 | 20 | 25 | 30 | 35 | 40 | 45 | 50 |
| 6 | 6 | 12 | 18 | 24 | 30 | 36 | 42 | 48 | 54 | 60 |
| 7 | 7 | 14 | 21 | 28 | 35 | 42 | 49 | 56 | 63 | 70 |
| 8 | 8 | 16 | 24 | 32 | 40 | 48 | 56 | 64 | 72 | 80 |
| 9 | 9 | 18 | 27 | 36 | 45 | 54 | 63 | 72 | 81 | 90 |
| 10 | 10 | 20 | 30 | 40 | 50 | 60 | 70 | 80 | 90 | 100 |

1. In Microsoft Word, go to View, and select the Tables and Borders toolbar.

2. Click on Insert Table.

3. In the message box, type 11 for number of columns and 11 for number of rows. Click on OK.

4. Starting with the upper left cell, highlight the entire table.

*(continued)*

5. Go to the Formatting toolbar and choose size 22, Arial Black font, and blue color.

6. Left click in the first cell in the upper left corner and type an "x."

7. Change the font color to red and type the numbers 1 through 10 in the cells in the top row.

8. Type the numbers 1 through 10 in the cells down the left column.

9. Now you are ready to fill in the products by multiplying each number on the side times (x) each number on the top and filling in the product in the cell where the column and row for that number cross.

10. Use the table to show that multiplication is repetitive addition. If you don't know some of the products, you may need to just keep adding the number to fill in the products. Ask your teacher to check your screen if you're not sure of a product.

12. Go to File and choose Save.

13. Save in My Documents with the title "[Your Name]'s Multiplication Table."

14. You can print your table and use it to learn the multiplication facts.

15. The saved table will be used later for other activities.

# The Commutative Property of Multiplication

*Objective:* To understand and model the commutative property of multiplication using the Microsoft Word Tables and Borders toolbar

| x | 1 | 2 | 3 | 4 | 5 | 6 | 7 | 8 | 9 | 10 |
|---|---|---|---|---|---|---|---|---|---|----|
| 1 | 1 | 2 | 3 | 4 | 5 | 6 | 7 | 8 | 9 | 10 |
| 2 | 2 | 4 | 6 | 8 | 10 | 12 | 14 | 16 | 18 | 20 |
| 3 | 3 | 6 | 9 | 12 | 15 | 18 | 21 | 24 | 27 | 30 |
| 4 | 4 | 8 | 12 | 16 | 20 | 24 | 28 | 32 | 36 | 40 |
| 5 | 5 | 10 | 15 | 20 | 25 | 30 | 35 | 40 | 45 | 50 |
| 6 | 6 | 12 | 18 | 24 | 30 | 36 | 42 | 48 | 54 | 60 |
| 7 | 7 | 14 | 21 | 28 | 35 | 42 | 49 | 56 | 63 | 70 |
| 8 | 8 | 16 | 24 | 32 | 40 | 48 | 56 | 64 | 72 | 80 |
| 9 | 9 | 18 | 27 | 36 | 45 | 54 | 63 | 72 | 81 | 90 |
| 10 | 10 | 20 | 30 | 40 | 50 | 60 | 70 | 80 | 90 | 100 |

- An operation on a set is *commutative* when it does not matter in which order the elements are combined.

1. Open the saved multiplication table document from the previous activity.

2. Look at row 4 and count across 3. You will find 12 ($4 \times 3 = 12$).

*(continued)*

**3.** Select 12 and click on the Highlight button on the Formatting toolbar to choose the color gray.

**4.** Look at row 3 and count across 4. You will find 12 again ($3 \times 4 = 12$).

**5.** Try other multiplication facts using the commutative property of multiplication and highlighting the products with the same color.

**6.** When you are finished, close the document without saving the changes.

# Multiplication Wheels

*Objective:* To develop proficiency with basic number combinations for multiplication using the Paint Tool Box and Color Box

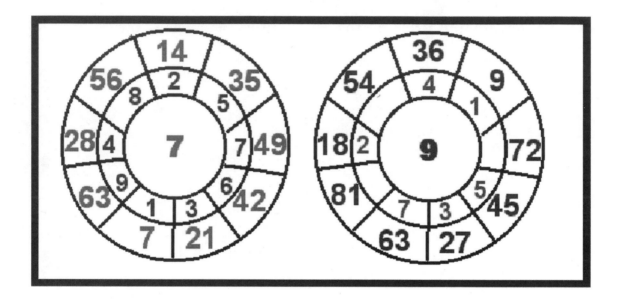

1. Click on the Ellipse button and choose transparent from the section at the bottom of the Tool Box. Click and drag (while holding down the Shift key) a medium-size circle.

2. Click and drag a smaller circle that will fit inside the medium circle, leaving a space large enough for a typed number.

3. Click and drag a circle to fit the same way inside the second circle.

4. Click on the Select button and choose transparent from the section at the bottom of the Tool Box. Select and move the second circle inside the first and the third circle inside the second.

5. Click on the Line button and drag lines dividing the two outside circles into nine equal parts. (Hint: First divide into thirds, then divide the thirds into three equal parts, or ninths.)

*(continued)*

6. Think of the number in your multiplication facts that is the most difficult for you to remember. Click on the Text button and drag a text box in the inside circle. Type the number (for example, 9).

7. Click on the Text button and drag a text box to an empty spot on the page. Type the numbers 1 through 9 (the factors).

8. Click on the Text button and drag a text box to another empty space on the page. Type the sums of adding your number to itself, then to the previous sum up to nine numbers (the multiples of that number; for example, for 9 the sums would be 18, 27, 36, 45, 54, 63, 72, and 81).

9. Click on the Select button to select and randomly move the numbers 1 through 9 to spaces on the middle circle.

10. Click on the Select button to select and move the multiples to their proper place on the wheel.

11. Work with a classmate to solve other multiplication wheels.

12. Try putting in the multiples and leaving the factor sections blank.

13. You can print your multiplication wheel and use it when you want to practice.

# Lattice Multiplication

*Objective:* To understand and use the distributive property of multiplication with the lattice method using the Paint Tool Box and Color Box

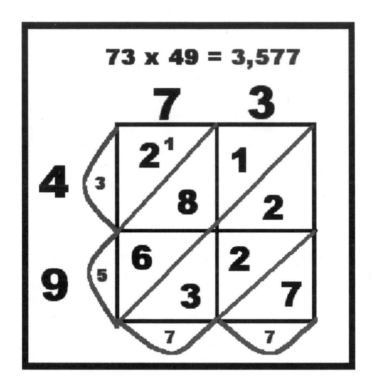

1. Click on the Line button and choose the thickness of the line from the section at the bottom of the Tool Box.

2. Click on the Rectangle button and click and drag a square on the page. (Hold down the Shift key while dragging the square. Release the mouse, then release the Shift key.)

3. Click on the Line button and click and drag lines to divide the square into four equal parts.

4. Choose red from the Color Box and divide each small square in half by drawing a diagonal red line from the upper right corner to the lower left corner.

*(continued)*

5. Click on the Brush button and choose the second option on the second row from the section at the bottom of the Tool Box. Draw a pocket at the end of each diagonal section.

6. Go to File and choose Save. Save in My Documents and title the file "Lattice Multiplication."

7. Click on the Text button and click and drag a text box to type the digits for your two-digit multiplication problem (for example, $49 \times 73$).

8. Click on the Select button and select the digits to move them above the columns and beside the row.

9. Click on the Text button and click and drag a text box to type the answers you get when you multiply each pair of digits (as if you were multiplying on a multiplication chart).

10. Click on the Select button and move the answers to their proper place on the chart with the tens digits on top of the red line and the ones digits below the red line.

11. Add the numbers in each diagonal section starting with the bottom right. Type the sums in a text box and move the sum inside the pocket at the end of the correct sections. (Carry numbers to the next level when needed.)

12. The answer to your problem is the number you get when you type the numbers in the pockets starting with the upper left-hand side as the thousands place.

13. Check your answer by multiplying the traditional way.

14. When closing the window, do not save your changes. You can use the blank lattice for other problems.

# Modeling Division

- - - - - - - - - - - - - - - ◆ - - - - - - - - - - - - - - -

*Objective:* To develop an understanding of the effects of dividing whole numbers using the Paint Tool Box and Color Box

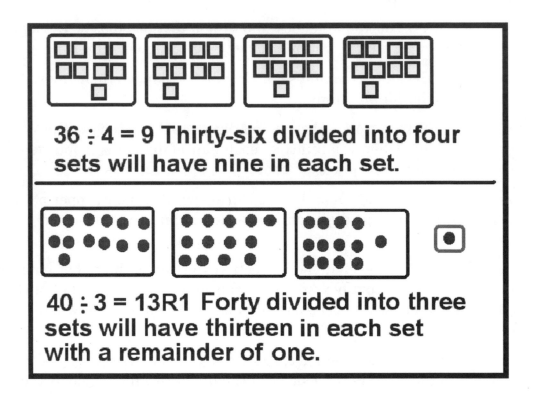

1. Click on the Rectangle button to create a small square tile. Click on the Fill With Color button, choose a color from the Color Box, and color the square.

2. Click on the Select button and select the square.

3. Go to Edit and choose Copy.

4. Go to Edit and choose Paste. Paste 34 more times (or to go faster, copy and paste in sets of two) for a total of 36 squares.

5. Click on the Ellipse button and drag (while holding down the Shift key) a small circle.

*(continued)*

6. Click on the Select button and copy and paste 39 circles for a total of 40 (or to go faster, copy and paste in sets of three).

7. Click on the Rounded Rectangle button and choose transparent from the section at the bottom of the Tool Box. Click and drag a medium-size rectangle.

8. Click on Select and copy and paste the rectangle to make four sets.

9. Still using Select, click on the square tiles, then drag them evenly into the sets. How many are in each set? ($36 \div 4 = 9$. There should be nine in each set.)

10. Click on the Rounded Rectangle button and make three sets for the circles.

11. Click on the Select button to move the circles evenly into the sets. Are any circles left? ($40 \div 3 = 13$ with a remainder of 1. There should be thirteen in each set with one left over.)

12. Use circles, squares, or other shapes to model other division problems.

# Rounding Whole Numbers on the Number Line

*Objective:* To develop an understanding of rounding whole numbers on the number line using the Paint Tool Box and Color Box

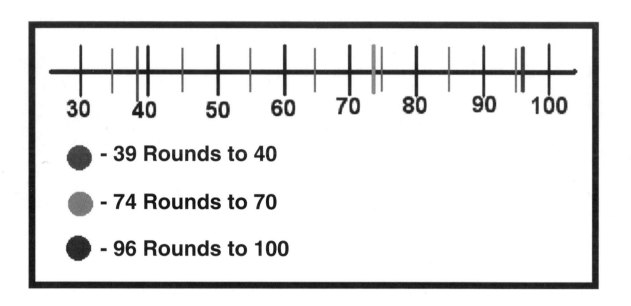

- ● - 39 Rounds to 40
- ● - 74 Rounds to 70
- ● - 96 Rounds to 100

1. Click on the Line button and choose the thickest size from the section at the bottom of the Tool Box. Click and drag a line across the screen.

2. Click on the Line button and choose a thinner size to click and drag vertical lines about an inch apart on the horizontal line.

3. Click on the Text button and click and drag a text box. Type the numbers from 30 to 100, counting by tens.

4. Click on the Select button and choose transparent from the section at the bottom of the Tool Box. Select and move the numbers in consecutive order to the bottom of each vertical line on the number line.

5. Click on the Line button and choose red from the Color Box. Click and drag vertical lines for 35, 45, 55, and so on.

*(continued)*

6. Choose green from the Color Box. Drag a vertical line where the number 39 would be on the number line. Is 39 closer to 40 or 30 on the number line? (It is greater than 35, so it is closer to 40.) The number 39 rounded to the nearest ten is 40.

7. Choose orange from the Color Box. Click and drag a vertical line where the number 74 would be on the number line. Is 74 closer to 70 or 80? (It is less than 75, so it is closer to 70.) The number 74 rounded to the nearest ten is 70.

8. Continue to change line colors to represent numbers on the number line. Remember that if the number in the ones place is 5 or greater, the tens will round up to the next ten.

9. Click on the Ellipse button and choose opaque from the section at the bottom of the Tool Box. Click and drag colored circles for each of your numbers.

10. Click on the Text button and click and drag text boxes next to the circles. Write the numbers in text boxes next to the corresponding colors.

11. Work with a classmate to locate and round other numbers on the number line.

# The Round Table

· · · · · · · · · · · · · · · · · · ◆ · · · · · · · · · · · · · · · · · ·

*Objective:* To develop an understanding of rounding whole numbers using the Microsoft Word Standard, Tables and Borders, and Formatting toolbars

| Number | Rounded to Thousands | Rounded to Hundreds | Rounded to Tens |
|---|---|---|---|
| 6,607 | 7,000 | 6,600 | 6,610 |
| 5,873 | 6,000 | 5,900 | 5,870 |
| 4,065 | 4,000 | 4,100 | 4,070 |
| 3,539 | 4,000 | 3,500 | 3,540 |
| 2,742 | 3,000 | 2,700 | 2,740 |

1. In Microsoft Word, go to View, and choose the Standard, Formatting, and Tables and Borders toolbars.

2. A table may be inserted two ways in Microsoft Word: (1) On the Standard toolbar, a table is inserted by dragging the number of columns and rows from the Insert Table button; (2) On the Tables and Borders toolbar, a table is inserted by typing the number of columns and rows in the message box from the Insert Table button.

3. Move the pointer outside to the left of the table until the arrow points to the top row. Left click to select the first row.

4. On the Formatting toolbar, choose Arial font, size 22, center align, and red color.

5. In the first column, type "Number."

*(continued)*

6. Press the Right Arrow key, Tab key, or left click in the next cell to move to the next cell to the right. In the second column, type "Rounded to Thousands."

7. In the third column, type "Rounded to Hundreds."

8. In the fourth column, type "Rounded to Tens."

9. Left click in the first cell in the second row to select the rest of the table. On the Formatting toolbar, choose Arial font, size 20, bold, center align, and black color.

10. In the Number column, type any five 4-digit numbers.

11. Move to the second column and round each number to the nearest thousand.

12. Continue to fill in the third and fourth columns by rounding the numbers to hundreds and tens.

13. On the Tables and Borders toolbar, choose the style, $4\frac{1}{2}$ pt. line weight, and a color for the border. Then click on the Outside Border button.

14. You can print your table and check it with a classmate.

# Odd and Even Numbers

◆

*Objective:* To identify and generate odd and even numbers using the Paint Tool Box and Color Box

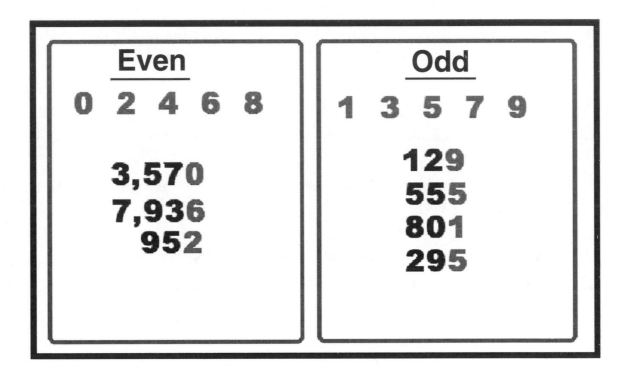

1. Click on the Text button and drag a text box on the screen.

2. Go to View and choose Text Toolbar.

3. On the Text Toolbar, choose Arial Black font, size 32, underlined, and black color from the Color Box.

4. Type "Even" and "Odd."

5. Drag another text box and choose red from the Color Box. Type the numbers 0 through 9.

6. Choose the Select button and choose transparent from the section at the bottom of the Tool Box. Select and move the numbers 0, 2, 4, 6, and 8 under the word "Even."

*(continued)*

7. Select and move the numbers 1, 3, 5, 7, and 9 under the word "Odd."

8. Click on the Rounded Rectangle button and choose green from the Color Box to drag two long green rectangles.

9. Click on the Select button. Select the word "Even" and the even numbers. Move them to the top of one rectangle.

10. Select the word "Odd" and the odd numbers. Move them to the top of the other rectangle.

11. Click on the Text button to click and drag a text box.

12. Go to View and choose Text Toolbar.

13. On the Text Toolbar, choose Arial Black font, size 28, and black color.

14. Type seven 3-digit or 4-digit numbers.

15. Click on the Fill With Color button and choose red from the Color Box. Color all the numbers in the ones place.

16. Determine if the number is even or odd. (Remember that a number is even if the number in the ones place is even. A number is odd if the number in the ones place is odd.)

17. Click on the Select button and select the whole numbers to move them inside the "Even" or "Odd" rectangle.

18. You can print your work and read the numbers to classmates. Ask them if the number is even or odd.

# Matho with Composite Numbers

························◆························

*Objective:* To describe classes of numbers according to characteristics, such as number of factors, using the Microsoft Word Formatting and Tables and Borders toolbars

| | | | | |
|---|---|---|---|---|
| 42 | 56 | 21 | 36 | 72 |
| 34 | 64 | 81 | 24 | 63 |
| 60 | 25 | FREE SPACE | 75 | 81 |
| 32 | 40 | 68 | 26 | 54 |
| 27 | 12 | 16 | 18 | 98 |

- A *composite number* is a number that has more than two factors.

- A *prime number* is a number that has only two factors.

1. In Microsoft Word, go to View, and choose the Tables and Borders toolbar.

2. Click on the Insert Table button. In the dialog box, type 5 for the number of columns and 5 for the number of rows.

3. Go to Edit and choose Select All.

Copyright © 2005 by John Wiley & Sons, Inc.

*(continued)*

4. On the Formatting toolbar, choose Arial font size 36, and black color. Your teacher will give you composite numbers from 1 to 100. Choose 24 of the numbers to type in the cells of the table. Leave the middle space blank.

5. Change the font size to 18 and type "Free Space" on the cell in the middle of the table.

6. Your teacher will draw one of the composite numbers from a bag. If the number called is on your table, choose the Highlight button on the Formatting toolbar. Left click in front of the number to drag a highlight.

7. If you get five highlights in a row, column, or diagonal, say "Matho." You are a winner!

# Hundred Board

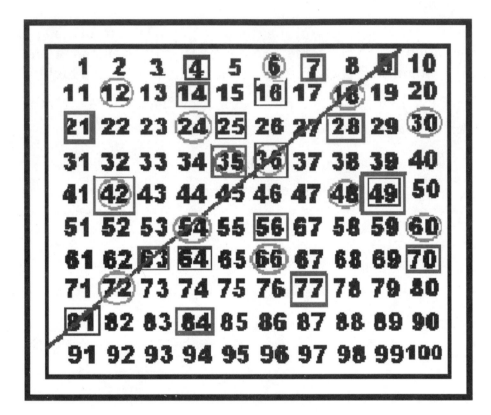

*Objective:* To describe classes of numbers according to characteristics, such as the multiples of a certain number, using the Paint Tool Box

- The *multiple* of a number is the result of that number multiplied by another counting number.

- A *square number* is the product of double factors.

1. Click on the Text button and drag a text box about the size of the screen.

2. On the toolbar, choose Arial font, size 22, and bold.

3. Putting two spaces between each number, type 1 through 10 in the first row, then press enter. Type 11 through 20 in the second row, then press enter. Type 21 through 30 in the third row, then press enter. Continue the pattern up to 100.

*(continued)*

**4.** When you have finished typing, left click outside the text box.

**5.** Click on the Select button and move the numbers in the first row so that they are above the ones place of the numbers on the second row.

**6.** Click on the line button and choose the third size from the section at the bottom of the Tool Box.

**7.** Click on the Rectangle button, then click and drag a rectangular frame around the numbers. You have constructed a "Hundred Board" that you can use to discover and draw conclusions about numbers and their relationships.

**8.** Go to File and choose Save.

**9.** Save under My Documents and title "[Your Name]'s Hundred Board."

**10.** Click on the Ellipse button and choose red from the Color Box. Click and drag a red circle around the number with 3 tens and 5 ones.

**11.** Click on the Line button and choose blue from the Color Box. Click and drag a line through the multiples of 9 up to 81.

**12.** Click on the Rectangle button and choose green from the Color Box. Click and drag a green rectangle around each multiple of 7.

**13.** Click on the Ellipse button and choose orange from the Color Box. Click and drag an orange circle around each multiple of 6.

**14.** Click on the Rectangle button and choose brown from the Color Box. Click and drag a brown rectangle around the square numbers.

**15.** Click on the Text button and drag a text box. Describe two properties you have learned about the number 49. Which number has a green rectangle and an orange circle? What principle does this represent and why? Look for other patterns and conclusions from this lesson.

**16.** Print your work and use your printed board to identify other multiples.

**17.** Close the document without saving your changes. You can use the "Hundred Board" for other activities.

# A Whole Written as a Fraction

◆ · · · · · · · · · · · · · · · · · · · · · ◆ · · · · · · · · · · · · · · · · · · · · ·

*Objective:* To recognize and generate an equivalent fraction of one whole using the Paint Tool Box and Color Box

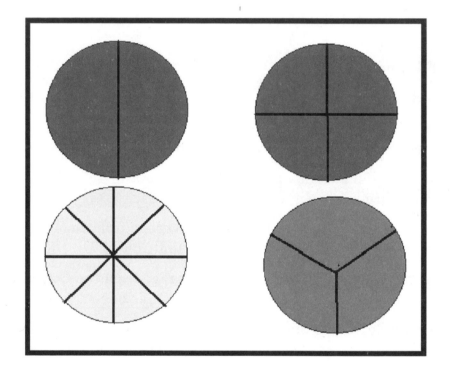

- The number of equal parts in a fraction is called the *denominator* (the number below the fraction bar).

- The number of equal parts being considered in a fraction is called the *numerator* (the number above the fraction bar).

- When the numerator and the denominator are the same, the fraction is equal to 1 (one whole).

**1.** Click on the Ellipse button and click and drag a circle (while holding down the Shift key) on the screen. The circle is one whole.

*(continued)*

2. Click on the Select button and choose transparent from the section at the bottom of the Tool Box.

3. Go to Edit and select Copy.

4. Go to Edit and select Paste.

5. Paste two more times for a total of four circles.

6. Click on the Fill With Color button and color one circle red, one blue, one yellow, and one orange.

7. Choose the Line button and the second line thickness from the section at the bottom of the Tool Box. Click and drag lines to divide the circles into equal parts: the red one into two parts (halves), the orange one into three parts (thirds), the blue one into four parts (fourths), and the yellow one into eight parts (eighths).

8. Click on the Text button and click and drag a text box next to each circle. Type fractions for the number of colored parts in each circle ($\frac{2}{2}$, $\frac{3}{3}$, and so on). Choose a color from the Color Box to type each fraction in the color of its circle.

9. Create another text box to write any conclusions you have made from this activity.

# Equivalent Fractions

*Objective:* To recognize and generate equivalent fractions for ½ using the Paint Tool Box and Color Box

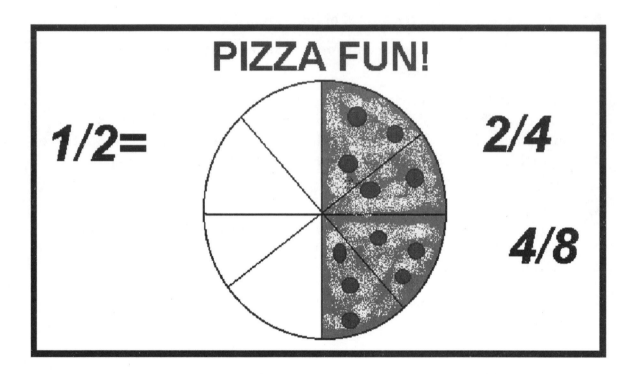

1. Click on the Ellipse button and click and drag (while holding down the Shift key) a large circle on the page.

2. Click on the Line button and click and drag a line that cuts your "pizza" circle into two equal parts.

3. Click on the Fill With Color button and choose red from the Color Box. Click on half of the pizza to spread the red "sauce."

4. Click on the Text button and click and drag a text box next to the pizza. Type the fraction for the part covered with sauce.

5. Click on the Line button and click and drag a line so that the pizza is divided into four equal parts.

*(continued)*

6. Click on the Text button and type another fraction (not $\frac{1}{1}$) for the part of the pizza covered with sauce and cheese ($\frac{2}{4}$).

7. Click on the Line button and draw two more lines to make eight equal parts.

8. Click on the Ellipse button and choose opaque from the section at the bottom of the Tool Box.

9. Choose brown from the Color Box and click and drag small circles for pepperoni.

10. Click on the Text button and type another fraction that describes the parts that have sauce, cheese, and pepperoni ($\frac{4}{8}$).

11. Click on the Text button and type equations for what you have learned.

# Comparing Fractions

*Objective:* To recognize and generate equivalent forms of commonly used fractions using the Paint Tool Box and Color Box

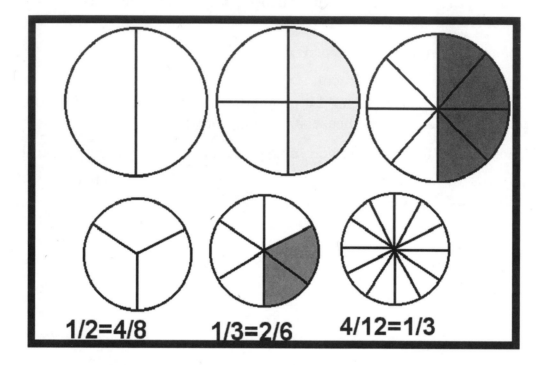

1/2=4/8    1/3=2/6    4/12=1/3

1. Click on the Line button and choose the second thickest size from the section at the bottom of the Tool Box.

2. Click on the Ellipse button and drag a medium-size circle (while holding down the Shift key).

3. Click on the Select button and choose transparent from the section at the bottom of the Tool Box. Select the circle.

4. Go to Edit and choose Copy.

5. Go to Edit and choose Paste.

6. Paste again to make a third circle.

*(continued)*

7. Click on the Line button and drag lines that divide one circle into halves, one into fourths, and one into eighths.

8. Click on the Select button and select the circle divided into fourths. Drag this circle over the circle divided into halves. (Do not click off the select box.)

9. How many fourths are the same as $\frac{1}{2}$?

10. Move the fourths circle back to its original position.

11. Click on the Text button and drag a text box on the page. Type $\frac{1}{2} = \frac{2}{4}$.

12. Compare fourths to eighths in the same manner and type the fractions that are equivalent.

13. Construct, compare, and record equivalent fractions using thirds, sixths, and twelfths. You may also use the Fill With Color button to compare equivalent fractions.

# Improper Fractions and Mixed Numerals

··················· ◆ ·······················

*Objective:* To develop an understanding of the relationship of an improper fraction to a mixed numeral using the Paint Tool Box and Color Box

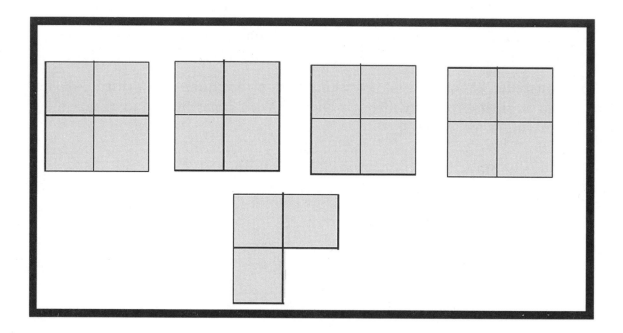

- An *improper fraction* is a fraction whose numerator is larger than its denominator.

- A *mixed numeral* is a whole number with a fraction.

1. Click on the Rectangle button and choose transparent from the section at the bottom of the Tool Box. Click and drag (while holding down the Shift key) a small square on the page.

2. Click on the Line button and drag lines that divide the square into four equal parts.

*(continued)*

3. Click on the Fill With Color button to color each quarter section blue ($\frac{4}{4}=1$).

4. Click on the Select button and choose transparent from the section at the bottom of the Tool Box. Select the square.

5. Go to Edit and choose Copy.

6. Go to Edit and choose Paste.

7. Move the pasted square next to the first square.

8. Continue to paste until you have four squares in a row.

9. How many fourths do you have? ($\frac{16}{4}$)

10. Go to Edit and choose Paste to paste another square.

11. Click on the Eraser button and erase one-fourth of the square.

12. How many fourths do you have? ($\frac{19}{4}$)

13. $\frac{19}{4}$ is an improper fraction.

14. Click on the Text button and drag a text box. Type the definitions of an improper fraction and a mixed numeral.

15. Explain why $\frac{16}{4}$ is a whole number.

16. Type another number for $\frac{19}{4}$. ($4\frac{3}{4}$)

# Adding Like Fractions

*Objective:* To develop an understanding of the addition of fractions as parts of a whole using the Paint Tool Box and Color Box

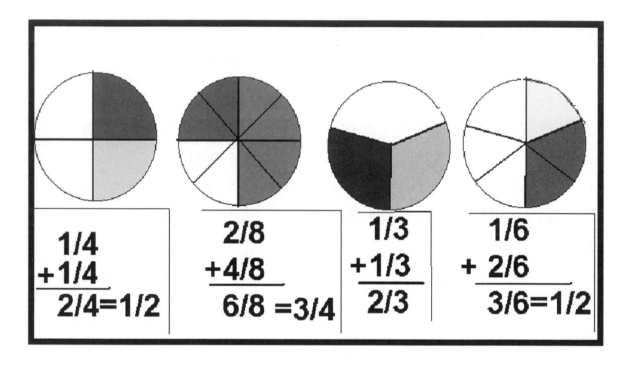

1. Click on the Ellipse button and choose transparent from the section at the bottom of the Tool Box. Click and drag a medium-size circle (while holding down the Shift key).

2. Click on the Select button and choose transparent from the section at the bottom of the Tool Box. Select the circle.

3. Go to Edit and choose Copy.

4. Go to Edit and choose Paste.

5. Move the pasted circle down on the screen.

6. Continue to paste until you have four circles.

*(continued)*

7. Click on the Line button and drag two lines to divide the first circle into four equal parts.

8. Click on the Fill With Color button and color one-quarter of the circle red and one-quarter blue.

9. Click on the Line button and drag four lines to divide the second circle into eight equal parts.

10. Click on the Fill With Color button to color two parts ($\frac{2}{8}$) blue and four parts ($\frac{4}{8}$) orange.

11. Click on the Line button and drag lines to divide the third circle into three equal parts.

12. Click on the Fill With Color button and color one part ($\frac{1}{3}$) brown and one part ($\frac{1}{3}$) green.

13. Click on the Line button and drag lines to divide the fourth circle into six equal parts.

14. Click on the Fill With Color button to color two parts ($\frac{2}{6}$) pink and one part ($\frac{1}{6}$) yellow.

15. Click on the Text button and type an addition problem for each circle showing the total number of parts. Explain why the denominators for the sums are the same as the addends.

16. Work with a partner to model addition of other like fractions.

# Subtracting Mixed Numerals

◆

*Objective:* To develop an understanding of renaming fractions when subtracting a mixed numeral from a whole number using the Paint Tool Box and Color Box

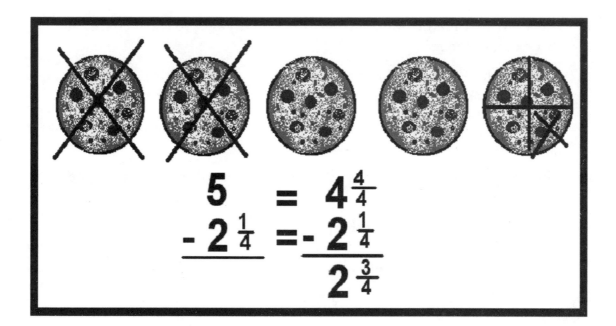

1. Right click on red and left click on black in the Color Box.

2. Click on the Ellipse button and choose opaque from the section at the bottom of the Tool Box. Drag a medium-size circle (while holding down the Shift key). The color red is the sauce on the pizza.

3. Click on the Airbrush button and choose yellow from the Color Box. Spray the yellow cheese on your pizza.

4. Right and left click on brown in the Color Box.

*(continued)*

5.  Click on the Ellipse button (still opaque) to drag small circles of pepperoni on your pizza. You may also use other Tool Box buttons to decorate your pizza.

6.  Click on the Select button and select the pizza.

7.  Go to Edit and choose Copy.

8.  Go to Edit and choose Paste.

9.  Continue to paste until you have five whole pizzas.

10. Use the pizza circles to answer this word problem: Mary had five pizzas for her party. The girls at her party ate $2\frac{1}{4}$ pizzas. How many were left?

11. Click on the Line button to divide one pizza into four equal parts.

12. Drag lines to cross out two whole pizzas and one-fourth of a third pizza. How many pizzas are left?

13. Click on the Text button and show how to solve the problem using numbers.

14. Write other word problems and exchange them with classmates.

# The Decimal Point

*Objective:* To recognize and read equivalent representations of decimals using the Paint Tool Box and Color Box

```
7  5  6  0  2  3
_____

5 32/100        5 ● 32
                  A
                  N
                  D
   five and thirty-two hundredths
```

1. Click on the Text button and drag a text box on the page. Choose size 36 from the Text Toolbar. Type the numbers 7, 5, 6, 0, 2, and 3, putting two spaces between each number.

2. Click on the Ellipse button and drag a small circle for the decimal point.

3. Click on the Fill With Color button to paint the decimal point red.

4. Click on the Text button and drag a small text box. Make the font size 12 and the type black.

5. Type "and" (pressing Enter on the keyboard after each letter).

6. Choose the Select button and select the word "and."

7. Move "and" under the red decimal point.

*(continued)*

8. The teacher or a classmate will say a fraction using the numbers that you typed (for example, five and thirty-two hundredths).

9. Click on the Select button and select the numbers that you need.

10. Go to Edit and choose Copy.

11. Go to Edit and choose Paste.

12. Move the numbers so that they are in the correct place value on either side of the decimal point (for example, 5.32).

13. Click on the Text button and drag a text box on the page. Type the decimal in words and as a fraction.

# Modeling Decimals

*Objective:* To develop an understanding of the place value structure of decimals in the base-ten number system using the Paint Tool Box and Color Box

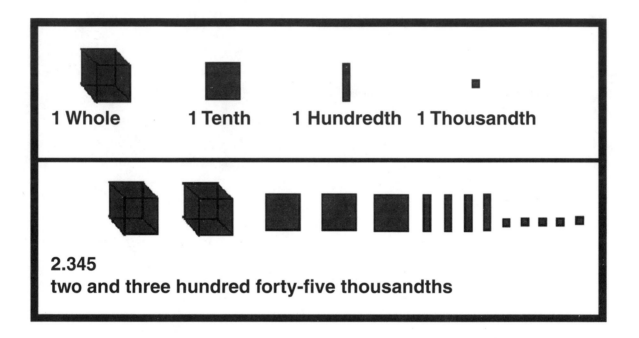

**1 Whole**　　**1 Tenth**　　**1 Hundredth**　**1 Thousandth**

**2.345**
**two and three hundred forty-five thousandths**

1. Click on the Rectangle button and drag a small square (while holding down the Shift key).

2. Click on the Select button and choose transparent from the section at the bottom of the Tool Box. Select the square.

3. Go to Edit and choose Copy.

4. Go to Edit and choose Paste.

5. Move the pasted square so that the top left corner is in the center of the original square.

6. Click on the Line button and make lines to connect the corners and form a cube. This will represent one whole (1).

*(continued)*

**7.** Go to Edit and choose Paste and move the pasted square down. This square will represent one-tenth (.1).

**8.** Click on the Rectangle button and drag a skinny rectangle the same height as the cube. This will represent one-hundredth (.01).

**9.** Click and drag (while holding down the Shift key) a small square (about one-tenth the size of the hundredth block). This will represent one-thousandth (.001).

**10.** Choose the Fill With Color button to color the blocks in your favorite color.

**11.** Model the decimal number given by the teacher by copying and pasting the blocks you drew.

**12.** Click on the Text button and drag a text box on the page. Type the decimal number you modeled in words.

**13.** Exchange decimal numbers with a classmate and model the number you received.

**14.** Model other decimal numbers.

# Comparing Decimals

· · · · · · · · · · · · · · · · · · · · ◆ · · · · · · · · · · · · · · · · · · · ·

*Objective:* To develop an understanding of comparing decimals using the Formatting toolbar in Microsoft Word

```
.007  <  .07
  .8  >  .08
 2.3  =  2.30
```

- The symbol > means is greater than.
- The symbol < means is less than.
- The symbol = means is equal to.

**1.** In Microsoft Word, go to View Toolbars and click on the Formatting toolbar.

**2.** Choose Arial font, size 36, bold.

**3.** Type the two decimals that the teacher writes on the chalkboard (for example, .007 and .07).

**4.** Click the cursor between the two decimals to insert the correct comparison symbol. (Hint: Think of the open end of the symbol as "Jaws" eating the greater number.)

**5.** Add a space on either side of the comparison symbol with the space bar.

**6.** Click and drag over the symbol and change the color to red on the Formatting toolbar.

*(continued)*

7. Type pairs of other decimals using the same digits in different places and insert the comparison symbol in red.

8. Work with a partner. Take turns putting in symbols for your partner's decimals.

# Ratios

*Objective:* To develop the concept of ratio using the Paint Tool Box and Color Box

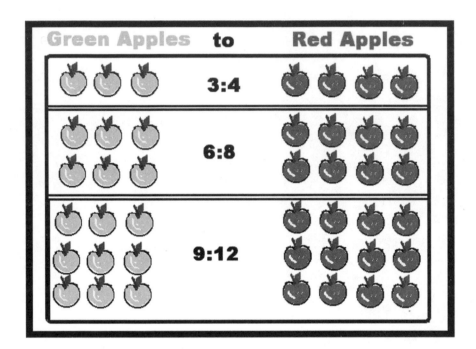

- A *ratio* is used to compare two or more quantities. A colon is used to separate the quantities.

- A *secondary ratio* is a multiple of a basic ratio.

- Two quantities are *in proportion* when corresponding parts are in the same ratio.

1. Use a model of a ratio to answer the following problem: The third-grade class at McHenry School decided to sell candy apples for a fund-raiser. They decided that for every three green candy apples made they would make four red candy apples. If the class made fifteen green apples, how many red apples did they make? How many candy apples did the class make in all?

*(continued)*

Copyright © 2005 by John Wiley & Sons, Inc.

2. Use the Ellipse, Pencil, or Brush button to draw a small apple.

3. Click on the Select button and choose transparent from the section at the bottom of the Tool Box. Select the apple.

4. Go to Edit and choose Copy.

5. Go to Edit and choose Paste.

6. Continue to paste until there are seven apples.

7. Click on Fill With Color and use the Color Box to color three apples green and four apples red.

8. Click on the Select button to select and separate the two sets of apples according to color.

9. Click on the Text button and drag a text box between the two sets. Type "3:4" (three to four ratio). This is the basic ratio (3:4) of green apples to red apples.

10. Click on the Rectangle button and choose transparent from the section at the bottom of the Tool Box. Click and drag a rectangle around the two groups of apples.

11. Click on Select and use Copy and Paste to double the green apples and double the red apples.

12. What is the ratio now? (6:8)

13. Use Copy and Paste to triple the sets of apples. What is the ratio now? (9:12)

14. Use the model to figure out what the ratio would be for fifteen green apples. (15:?)

15. Add the number of green apples sold to the number of red apples sold to find the total number of apples sold.

16. Work with a partner to create another basic ratio and construct secondary ratios.

# Constructing a
# 10 × 10 Grid

*Objective:* To construct a 10 × 10 grid using the Paint Tool Box and Color Box to be saved and used for math activities

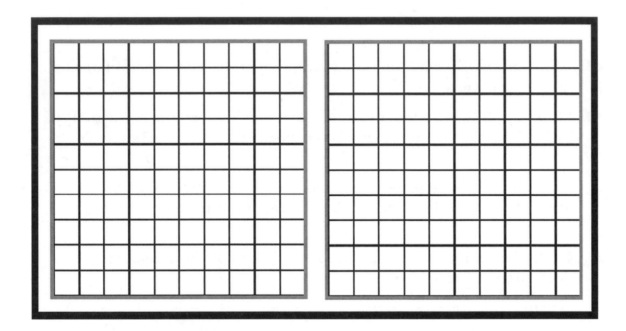

1. Click on the Rectangle button and choose transparent from the section at the bottom of the Tool Box. Click and drag (while holding down the Shift key) a small square.

2. Click on the Select button and choose transparent from the section at the bottom of the Tool Box. Select the square.

3. Go to Edit and choose Copy.

4. Go to Edit and choose Paste.

5. Move the pasted square to the right of the original so that the sides are touching.

*(continued)*

6. Continue to paste until there are ten connected squares in a row.

7. Select the row of ten squares.

8. Go to Edit and choose Copy.

9. Go to Edit and choose Paste.

10. Move the pasted row to connect under the original.

11. Continue to paste until there are ten rows.

12. Click on the Rectangle button and choose any color from the Color Box.

13. Click and drag a border around the grid.

14. Click on the Select button and select the grid.

15. Go to Edit and choose Copy.

16. Go to Edit and choose Paste.

17. Move the pasted grid next to the original. These are 10 × 10 grids that may be used for many math activities.

18. Go to File and choose Save.

19. In the message box, type in the title "[Your Name]'s 10 × 10 Grid."

20. Choose Save. The document is saved and may be opened for activities (such as the next one in this book) that require a grid.

# Modeling Percents on 10 × 10 Grids

........................................◆........................................

*Objective:* To recognize and generate equivalent forms of fractions, decimals, and percents using the Paint Tool Box and Color Box

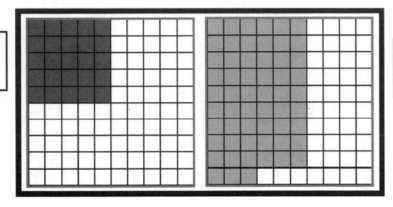

- A *percent* is a ratio that means per hundred, or out of a hundred.

- When a percent is written as a fraction, the denominator is 100.

1. Open the document titled "[Your Name]'s 10 × 10 Grid" (created in the previous activity).

2. Click on the Select button and choose transparent from the section at the bottom of the Tool Box. Select the two grids.

3. Go to Edit and choose Copy. Now the two grids are stored on the clipboard and can be pasted later. The grids have an area of 100 square units. Each square is $\frac{1}{100}$ of the grid. The fraction $\frac{1}{100}$ written as a decimal is .01.

4. Click on the Fill With Color button and choose a color from the Color Box. Color in a 5 × 5 area on the first grid. What fraction of the grid is colored? ($\frac{1}{4}$) How many of the squares are colored? (25) This may be written as $\frac{25}{100}$. Note that $\frac{1}{4} = \frac{25}{100}$ and $\frac{25}{100} = 25\%$.

*(continued)*

5. Click on Text button and drag a text box next to the grid. Type 25% in the text box.

6. Choose the Fill With Color button to color $\frac{57}{100}$ of the second grid. What percent is shaded? (57%) What is the ratio? (57:100)

7. Click on the Text button and drag a text box next to the second grid. Type 57% in the text box.

8. Click on the Select button and select all the images that you created. Choose Delete on the keyboard.

9. Go to Edit and choose Paste.

10. Color in new percents on the new grids and type them as fractions, decimals, ratios, and percents.

11. When closing the document, do not save the changes.

# Combinations

◆

*Objective:* To investigate, represent, and solve combination problems using the Paint Tool Box and Color Box

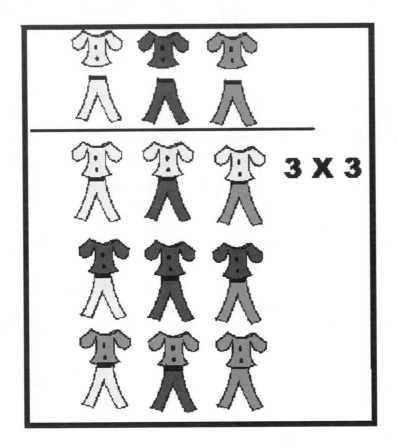

1. Use modeling to solve the following problem: Mary has a yellow blouse and pants set, an orange set, and a green set. How many different outfits can she wear using different combinations of blouses and pants?

2. Click on the Brush or Pencil button and use it to draw a blouse.

3. Draw a pair of pants under the blouse. (Leave some space between the blouse and the pants.)

4. Click on the Select button and select the blouse.

*(continued)*

**5.** Go to Edit and choose Copy.

**6.** Go to Edit and choose Paste.

**7.** Move the pasted blouse beside the original.

**8.** Paste one more blouse to make a row of three blouses.

**9.** Select the pants.

**10.** Go to Edit and choose Copy.

**11.** Go to Edit and choose Paste.

**12.** Move the pasted pants under the second blouse. (Leave some space between the pants and the blouse.)

**13.** Paste one more pair of pants and move it under the third blouse.

**14.** Click on the Fill With Color button and color one blouse and pants set yellow, one set green, and one set orange.

**15.** Click on the Line button and drag a line under the three outfits.

**16.** Copy and paste the blouses and pants below the line to form as many different outfits as you can. Think of a way to organize the problem.

**17.** Add another blouse and pants set and make it a different color. How many outfits can you make? Do you see a rule for finding combinations without drawing?

**18.** Click on the Text button and drag a text box to type your conclusions.

# Adding Integers

*Objective:* To develop an understanding of adding integers using the Paint Tool Box and Color Box

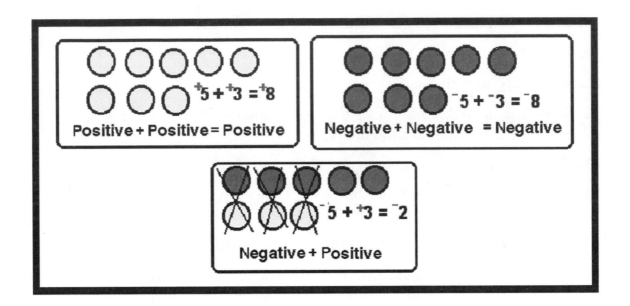

1. In the Color Box, left click on black and right click on yellow.

2. Click on the Ellipse button and choose opaque from the bottom of the Tool Box. Click and drag (while holding down the Shift key) a small yellow circle outlined in black. (This will be the positive integer chip.)

3. Click on the Select button and choose opaque from the section at the bottom of the Tool Box. Select the chip.

4. Go to Edit and choose Copy.

5. Go to Edit and choose Paste.

6. Move the chip next to the original.

7. Continue to paste until you have a total of five chips in a row.

8. Paste three more yellow chips below the first row of chips.

9. Positive five plus positive three equals positive eight ($^+5 + ^+3 = ^+8$).

*(continued)*

10. Click on Select and select the set of eight chips.

11. Go to Edit and choose Copy.

12. Go to Edit and choose Paste.

13. Move the second set of chips next to the first.

14. Click on the Fill With Color button and choose red from the Color Box. Change the color of all the chips in the second set to red. (These will be the negative chips.)

15. Negative five plus negative three equals negative eight ($^-5 + {}^-3 = {}^-8$).

16. Combining negative chip and a positive chip makes zero. ($^-1 + {}^+1 = 0$)

17. Paste eight more chips and move them below the other chips.

18. Color five chips in the new set red and three yellow.

19. Click on the Line button and choose black from the Color Box. Drag lines to cross out pairs of yellow and red chips. How many are left? Are they positive or negative? ($^-2$)

20. Add more yellow and red chips.

21. Cross out the zeros.

22. Click on the Text button and drag a text box. Type the equations for your findings.

23. Type the rules for adding positive plus positive, negative plus negative, and positive plus negative.

# Subtracting Integers

◆ ⋯⋯⋯⋯⋯⋯⋯⋯⋯⋯⋯⋯⋯⋯⋯⋯⋯ ◆ ⋯⋯⋯⋯⋯⋯⋯⋯⋯⋯⋯⋯⋯⋯⋯⋯⋯

*Objective:* To develop an understanding of subtracting integers using the Paint Tool Box and Color Box

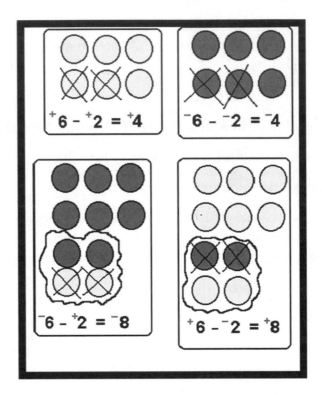

1. Left click on black and right click on yellow in the Color Box.

2. Click on the Ellipse button and choose opaque from the section at the bottom of the Tool Box. Click and drag (while holding down the Shift key) a small yellow circle outlined in black. (This will be your positive integer chip.)

3. Click on the Select button and choose opaque from the section at the bottom of the Tool Box. Select the chip.

4. Go to Edit and choose Copy.

5. Go to Edit and choose Paste.

*(continued)*

**6.** Continue to paste until you have six positive chips.

**7.** Click on the Line button and cross out two positive chips. How many chips are left? Are they positive?

**8.** Click on the Text button and drag a text box under the chips. Type $^+6 - {}^+2 = {}^+4$.

**9.** Paste six more chips.

**10.** Click on the Fill With Color button and choose red from the Color Box. Color these six chips red. (These will be your negative chips.)

**11.** Click on the Line button and cross out two negative chips. How many are left?

**12.** Click on the Text button and drag a text box under the chips. Type $^-6 - {}^-2 = {}^-4$.

**13.** Paste six more chips.

**14.** Choose the Fill With Color button to color the chips red.

**15.** Subtract two positive chips. Because there are no positives, you must add two zeros (2 pairs with a negative and a positive chip).

**16.** Click on the Line button. Now cross out the two positive chips. What is left? ($^-8$)

**17.** Click on the Text button and drag a text box under the chips. Type $^-6 - {}^+2 = {}^-8$.

**18.** Paste six more positive (yellow) chips.

**19.** Subtract two negative chips. Because there are no negatives, you must add two zeros (2 pairs with a negative and a positive chip).

**20.** Click on the Line button. Now cross out the two negatives. What is left? ($^+8$)

**21.** Click on the Text button and drag a text box under the chips. Type $^+6 - {}^-2 = {}^+8$.

**22.** Work with a classmate to model more subtracting integers.

# Section 3

# MEASUREMENT

# Telling Time

*Objective:* To understand the properties of a standard clock and to identify time on a standard and digital clock using the Paint Tool Box and Color Box

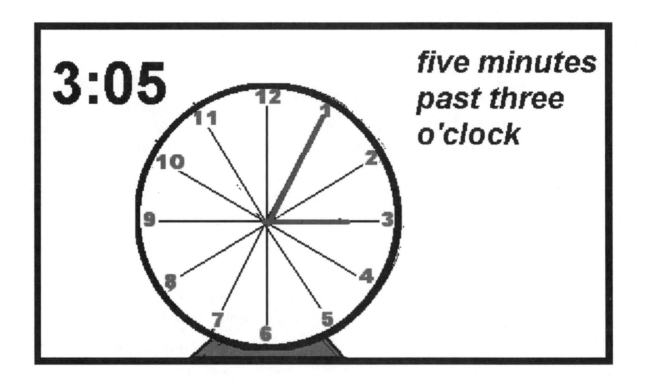

1. Click on the Line button and choose the thickest size from the section at the bottom of the Tool Box.

2. Click on the Ellipse button and choose transparent from the section at the bottom of the Tool Box. Click and drag (while holding down the Shift key) a medium-size circle.

3. Click on the Line button and choose the thinnest size. Click and drag lines that divide the circle into twelve equal parts. (Hint: First divide the circle into four equal parts, then divide each fourth into three equal parts.)

4. Click on the Text button and drag a text box.

*(continued)*

**5.** Go to View and choose Text Toolbar.

**6.** Choose Arial font, size 14, red, and bold.

**7.** In the text box, type numbers 1 through 12, leaving two spaces between each number.

**8.** Click on the Select button and choose opaque from the section at the bottom of the Tool Box. Select and move each number to its proper place on the clock.

**9.** Go to File and choose Save.

**10.** Save with the title "[Your Name]'s Clock."

**11.** Click on the Line button and choose the thickest size from the section at the bottom of the Tool Box. Choose brown from the Color Box.

**12.** Drag lines to form the hour and minute hands that show the time given to you by your teacher or a classmate. What kind of angle did the hands make?

**13.** Go to Edit and choose Undo twice to erase the hands on the clock. Now you are ready to set a new time.

**14.** Click on the Text button and drag a text box. Type the time in the digital form and the angle the hands make for that time (3:05, acute angle).

**15.** Looking at the clock, think about why we say things like "a quarter after" or "a quarter to" when telling time.

**16.** Close the document without saving your changes.

# Elapsed Time

· · · · · · · · · · · · · · · · · · · ◆ · · · · · · · · · · · · · · · · · · · ·

*Objective:* To develop the understanding of elapsed time using the Paint Tool Box and Color Box

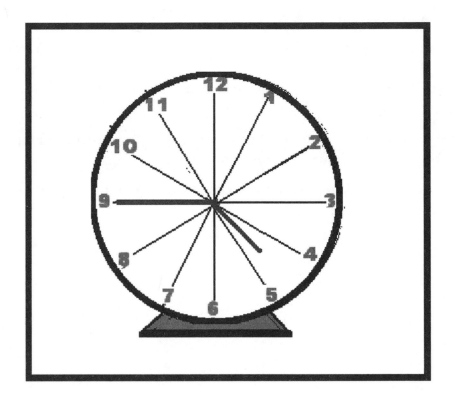

- Elapsed time is the amount of time that has passed between two events.

**1.** Open the document titled "[Your Name]'s Clock" from the previous activity.

**2.** Click on the Select button and choose transparent from the section at the bottom of the Tool Box. Select the clock.

**3.** Go to Edit and choose Copy.

**4.** Go to File and choose New.

*(continued)*

5. Go to Edit and choose Paste.

6. Move the pasted clock down the screen.

7. Click on the Line button and choose the thickest size from the section at the bottom of the Tool Box. Choose green from the Color Box.

8. Click and drag the clock hands to show 4:45.

9. How much time elapsed since 1:00? (The time is 4:45, or 45 minutes after 4:00. How many hours from 1:00 to 4:00 [3] and how many minutes from 4:00 to 4:45 [45]? The elapsed time from 1:00 to 4:45 is 3 hours 45 minutes.)

10. Click on the Text button and drag a text box to record the elapsed time. (1:00 to 4:45 is 3 hours 45 minutes.)

11. Work with a partner to create elapsed time word problems for other classmates to solve.

# The Ruler of Measurement

◆

*Objective:* To develop an understanding of measuring and reading customary units of length using the Paint Tool Box and Color Box

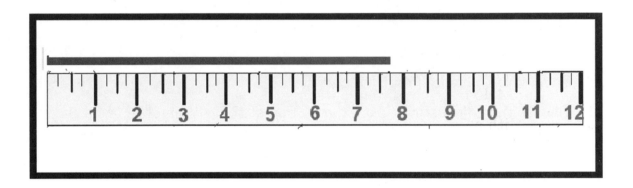

- A ruler is used to measure the length of an object. A foot ruler is divided into twelve equal parts (twelfths). Each twelfth can be divided into four equal parts (fourths). (Remember that $\frac{2}{4} = \frac{1}{2}$.)

1. Click on the Rectangle button and drag a rectangle that looks like a ruler.

2. Click on the Fill With Color button and color the ruler yellow.

3. Click on the Line button and choose the thickest line from the section at the bottom of the Tool Box. Drag a short line (about half the width of the ruler in length) to mark one-half of the ruler's length.

4. Use the same-size line to divide the ruler into twelve equal units. (Hint: Divide each half into six equal parts.)

5. Click on the Text button and drag a text box. In the Text Toolbar, choose Arial font, size 16, and bold. Choose red from the Color Box. Type the numbers from 1 through 12, leaving two spaces between each number.

*(continued)*

6. Click on the Select button and choose transparent from the section at the bottom of the Tool Box. Select and move each number under the correct line on the ruler.

7. Click on the Line button and choose the third thickness size from the section at the bottom of the Tool Box. Choose black from the Color Box. Drag a short line in the middle of each unit (this is one-half unit).

8. Choose the first thickness size from the section at the bottom of the Tool Box and drag a line in the middle of each half unit (this is one-fourth unit).

9. Go to File and choose Save.

10. Save with the title "[Your Name]'s Ruler."

11. Choose the thickest line from the section at the bottom of the Tool Box. Choose green from the Color Box. Drag a green line that is 7 units long, using your ruler as a guide.

12. Go to Edit and select Undo to erase the line.

13. Now drag a line that is $7\frac{3}{4}$ units.

14. Working with a partner, continue to drag lines of different measurements.

15. When you close the document, do not save your changes.

# Constructing and Interpreting a Calendar

*Objective:* To construct and interpret a calendar using the Microsoft Word Standard toolbar, Formatting toolbar, Drawing toolbar, and the Paint Tool Box and Color Box

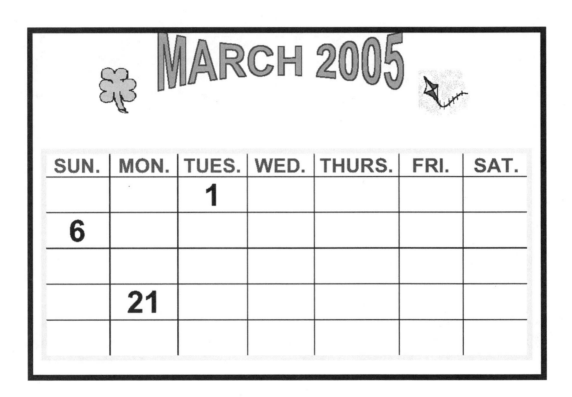

| SUN. | MON. | TUES. | WED. | THURS. | FRI. | SAT. |
|------|------|-------|------|--------|------|------|
|      |      | **1** |      |        |      |      |
| **6** |     |       |      |        |      |      |
|      |      |       |      |        |      |      |
|      | **21** |    |      |        |      |      |
|      |      |       |      |        |      |      |

1. On the Standard toolbar in Microsoft Word, choose the Insert Table button.

2. In the Message Box choose 7 columns and 6 rows.

3. Left click in the first cell and highlight the first row of the table.

4. Go to the Formatting toolbar and choose Arial font, size 18, bold, and red color.

*(continued)*

5. Click in each cell to type the abbreviations for the days of the week in capital letters.

6. Click on the first cell in the second row and highlight the rest of the table.

7. Go to the Formatting toolbar and choose Arial font, size 16, bold, and black color.

8. The first of March in 2005 is a Tuesday. Find the cell in the second row and type in 1.

9. Find the third Monday on the calendar. Type in 21.

10. Mary goes to church on the first Sunday in March. Type in the date. (6)

11. Complete your calendar by typing the other dates in their correct places.

12. Open Microsoft Paint and draw a small picture to represent the month of March. For example, a kite, a shamrock, or spring flowers.

13. Click on the Select button and select the picture.

14. Go to Edit and choose Copy.

15. Go back to your calendar on the Word screen.

16. Click the cursor on the screen below the calendar.

17. Go to Edit and choose Paste to paste your artwork.

18. Work with a classmate to ask questions about your calendar such as: What is the date of the third Wednesday in March? How many Sundays are there in March? What is the date two weeks after March 3?

# Constructing a Geoboard

- - - - - - - - - - - - - - - ◆ - - - - - - - - - - - - - - -

*Objective:* To construct a computer geoboard to use for measurement and geometry activities using the Paint Tool Box and Color Box

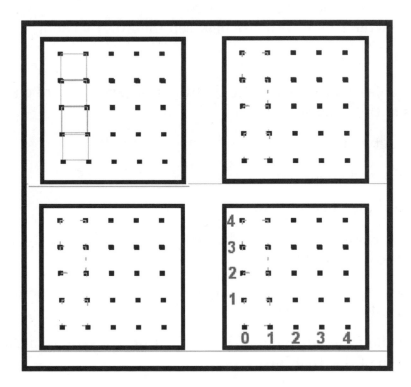

1. Click on the Text button and drag a long text box.

2. On the Text Toolbar, choose Arial Black font, size 28.

3. Choose black from the Color Box.

4. Type five periods, leaving two spaces between each period.

5. Click on the Select button and choose transparent from the section at the bottom of the Tool Box. Select the row of dots.

6. Go to Edit and choose Copy.

7. Click on the Line button and choose the thinnest size from the section at the bottom of the Tool Box.

*(continued)*

**8.** Choose the light gray color in the Color Box.

**9.** Click on the Rectangle button and choose transparent from the section at the bottom of the Tool Box.

**10.** Place the cursor on the first dot so that the center of the cross is over the dot. Drag (while holding down the Shift key) a square in which the top edge is the length of the space between the first two dots.

**11.** Go to Edit and choose Paste.

**12.** Move the pasted row of dots so that the first two dots are on the bottom corners of the square.

**13.** Select the two rows of dots.

**14.** Go to Edit and choose Copy.

**15.** Go to Edit and choose Paste.

**16.** Move the pasted dots so that the first row overlaps (evenly) the second row of the copied dots.

**17.** Paste two more times and overlap the rows as before. You have constructed a $4 \times 4$ unit grid.

**18.** Click on the Line button and choose the thickest size from the section at the bottom of the Tool Box.

**19.** Choose black from the Color Box.

**20.** Click on the Rectangle button and choose transparent from the section at the bottom of the Tool Box. Drag a square around the $4 \times 4$ unit grid. Choose the Eraser button to erase the light gray lines outside the dots. This is a geoboard.

**21.** Click on the Select button and select the geoboard.

**22.** Go to Edit and choose Copy.

**23.** Go to Edit and choose Paste. Paste four geoboards.

**24.** Go to File and choose Save.

**25.** Save the document with the title "[Your Name]'s Geoboard."

# Area and Perimeter
# of a Rectangle

*Objective:* To develop an understanding of and use formulas for finding the area and perimeter of rectangles using the Paint Tool Box and Color Box

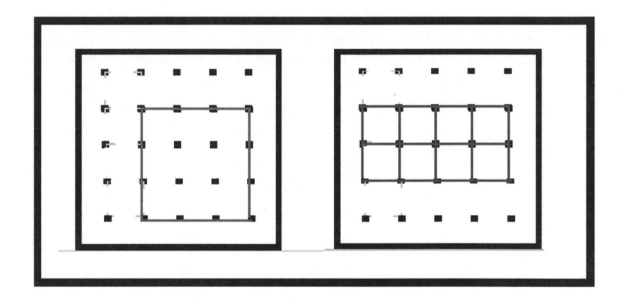

- The *perimeter* is the length of the distance around the outside of a two-dimensional figure or shape. The formula for the perimeter of a rectangle is $P = 2(l + w)$, where $l$ = length and $w$ = width.

- The *area* is the number of square units inside a two-dimensional figure or shape. The formula for the area of a rectangle is $A = l \times w$.

- Remember that a square is a type of rectangle, so the formulas are the same.

1. Open the geoboard document you created in the previous activity.

2. Click on the Select button and choose transparent from the section at the bottom of the Tool Box. Select the geoboard.

*(continued)*

3. Go to Edit and choose Copy.

4. Close the original document.

5. Go to File and choose New.

6. Go to Edit and choose Paste.

7. Click on the line button and choose the second thickness from the section at the bottom of the Tool Box. Click and drag lines to draw a square and a rectangle by connecting some of the dots on the geoboard.

8. Click on the Text button and drag a text box. Record the length and width of your rectangles. Type the formulas for the area and the perimeter of a rectangle. Use the formulas to find and record the perimeter (in units) and the area (in square units) of each shape.

9. Check the formula for perimeter by counting the units around your rectangles. Check the formula for area by counting the number of square units inside your rectangles.

# Four Square Polygons

*Objective:* To generate and identify regular and irregular polygons with areas of 4 square units using the Paint Tool Box and Color Box

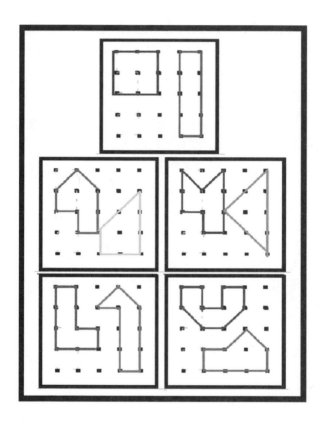

- A *polygon* is a plane shape (has all its points in one plane) bounded by only straight lines.

- A *regular polygon* has sides that are all the same length and angles that are all the same size.

- An *irregular polygon* does not have equal sides and equal angles.

1. Open the geoboard document that you created in the activity on page 99.

2. Click on the Select button and choose transparent from the section at the bottom of the Tool Box. Select a geoboard.

*(continued)*

**3.** Go to Edit and choose Copy.

**4.** Close the original document.

**5.** Go to File and choose New.

**6.** Go to Edit and choose Paste.

**7.** Click on the Line button and choose the third size from the section at the bottom of the Tool Box. Draw at least ten regular or irregular polygons that each have an area of 4 square units. Make each polygon a different color using the Color Box. (Note: A diagonal line will make a half unit.)

# ABC Area

*Objective:* To develop strategies for calculating the area of an irregular polygon using the Paint Tool Box and Color Box

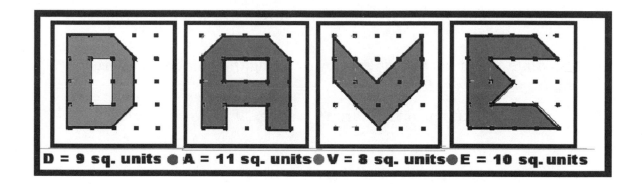

D = 9 sq. units ● A = 11 sq. units ● V = 8 sq. units ● E = 10 sq. units

1. Open the geoboard document that you created in the activity on page 99.

2. Click on the Select button and select the geoboard.

3. Go to Edit and choose Copy.

4. Close the original document.

5. Go to File and choose New.

6. Go to Edit and choose Paste.

7. Click on the Line button and choose the second or third size from the section at the bottom of the Tool Box.

8. Drag lines between dots (while holding down the Shift key) on the geoboard to form the first letter (capital) of your name. Connect the dots with straight lines or diagonal lines (to form half units). Remember to make the lines touch so that the letter-shaped polygon is closed.

9. Click on the Fill With Color button and choose any color you want from the Color Box. Click inside the letter to color it.

10. Go to Edit and choose Paste to paste another geoboard. Move the pasted geoboard next to the first.

*(continued)*

**11.** Click on the Line button and drag lines (while holding down the Shift key) between the dots on your geoboard to form the second letter in your name.

**12.** Click on the Fill With Color button and choose a different color from the Color Box to fill in this letter.

**13.** Continue to paste geoboards and draw lines until you have completed your first name.

**14.** Calculate the area of each letter by counting the number of colored square units in the letter.

**15.** Click on the Text button and drag a text box. Type your results.

# Estimating Perimeter and Area

*Objective:* To develop strategies and use benchmarks to estimate measurements using the Paint Tool Box and Color Box

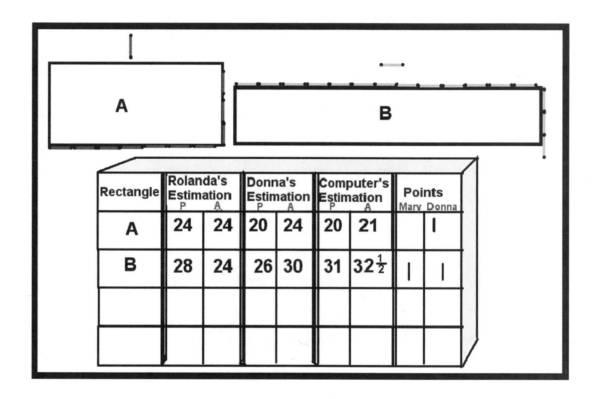

| Rectangle | Rolanda's Estimation | | Donna's Estimation | | Computer's Estimation | | Points | |
|---|---|---|---|---|---|---|---|---|
| | P | A | P | A | P | A | Mary | Donna |
| A | 24 | 24 | 20 | 24 | 20 | 21 | | I |
| B | 28 | 24 | 26 | 30 | 31 | 32½ | I | I |
| | | | | | | | | |
| | | | | | | | | |

**1.** Click on the Line button and choose the third size from the section at the bottom of the Tool Box. Click and drag a line the width of the tip of your pointer finger. (You may lightly touch the screen with your pointer finger to measure.) This width is about 1 centimeter long.

**2.** Click on the Line button and choose the thickest size from the section at the bottom of the Tool Box. Click a dot at the end of each line. This will be your unit of measurement.

**3.** You may make a table by using the Rectangle and Line buttons to keep score.

*(continued)*

4. Click on the Rectangle button and drag two medium-size rectangles. Click on the Text button and drag a text box in the rectangles. Label one "A" and the other "B."

5. Work with a partner to come up with estimates of the perimeter and the area of each rectangle in the unit that you created. Record the estimates in the table.

6. Click on the Select button and choose transparent from the section at the bottom of the Tool Box. Select the unit of measurement.

7. Go to Edit and choose Copy.

8. Go to Edit and choose Paste.

9. Paste the unit of measurement along the length of rectangle A.

10. Continue to paste units end to end along the length of the rectangle.

11. With the unit still selected, measure the width of the rectangle by going to Image and choosing Flip/Rotate and 90°.

12. Go to Edit and choose Copy.

13. Go to Edit and choose Paste.

14. Continue to paste until you have measured the width with the units.

15. Count the number of units for the length and for the width.

16. Calculate the perimeter and the area of rectangle A.

17. Record the measurements in the table.

18. Compare your estimates to the measurements you made. The person with the closest estimate without going over the computer estimate receives one point. (Count one point for perimeter and one point for area.)

19. Continue by making estimates and measuring rectangle B.

# Investigating the Formula for the Area of a Triangle

◆

*Objective:* To develop an understanding of and use the formula for the area of a triangle using the Paint Tool Box and Color Box

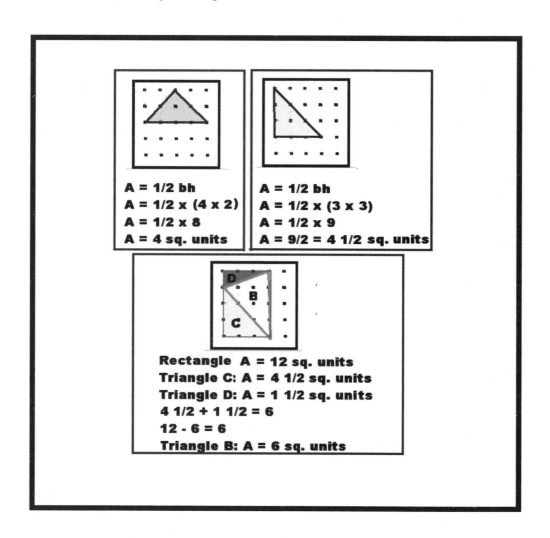

A = 1/2 bh
A = 1/2 x (4 x 2)
A = 1/2 x 8
A = 4 sq. units

A = 1/2 bh
A = 1/2 x (3 x 3)
A = 1/2 x 9
A = 9/2 = 4 1/2 sq. units

Rectangle  A = 12 sq. units
Triangle C: A = 4 1/2 sq. units
Triangle D: A = 1 1/2 sq. units
4 1/2 + 1 1/2 = 6
12 - 6 = 6
Triangle B: A = 6 sq. units

- The formula for the area of a triangle is $A = \frac{1}{2}bh$, where $b$ = base and $h$ = height.

- A *right triangle* is a triangle that has one right angle.

*(continued)*

## Investigating the Formula for the Area of a Triangle *(continued)*

- An *acute triangle* is a triangle that has three acute angles.

- An *obtuse triangle* is a triangle that has one obtuse angle.

1. Open the geoboard document that you created in the activity on page 99.

2. Click on the Select button and select the geoboard.

3. Go to Edit and choose Copy.

4. Close the original document.

5. Go to File and choose New.

6. Go to Edit and choose Paste.

7. Click on the Line button and choose the thickest size from the section at the bottom of the Tool Box.

8. Choose a color from the Color Box.

9. Draw a right triangle by connecting dots on the geoboard.

10. Count the number of squares in your triangle. The area of the triangle is the total number of square units. Remember that two halves equal one whole.

11. Go to Edit and choose Paste to paste another geoboard.

12. Draw a different-size right triangle and count the square units.

13. Go to Edit and choose Paste to paste another geoboard.

14. Draw a third right triangle that is different from the others and count the square units.

15. Calculate the *product* of the number of units in the base times the number of units in the height for each triangle. Compare the result to the number of counted squares in each triangle. What do you notice? The product of the base times the height is twice the number of counted squares, which means that $A = \frac{1}{2}b \times h$.

16. Paste another geoboard.

17. Draw an acute or obtuse triangle on the geoboard.

*(continued)*

**18.** Click on the Rectangle button and choose transparent from the section at the bottom of the Tool Box. Drag a rectangle around the triangle to form two right triangles inside the rectangle.

**19.** Click on the Fill With Color button and color each right triangle a different color.

**20.** Compute the area of the rectangle.

**21.** Compute the area of the right triangles.

**22.** Subtract the area of the two right triangles from the area of the rectangle. The area of the obtuse or acute triangle is the difference between the rectangle area and the sum of the area of the right triangles.

**23.** Work with a partner to draw more triangles and compute the areas.

# Volume of a Rectangular Prism

· · · · · · · · · · · · · · · · · · · · · ◆ · · · · · · · · · · · · · · · · · · · ·

*Objective:* To calculate and represent the formula for the volume of a rectangular prism using the Microsoft Word Drawing toolbar and the Paint Tool Box and Color Box

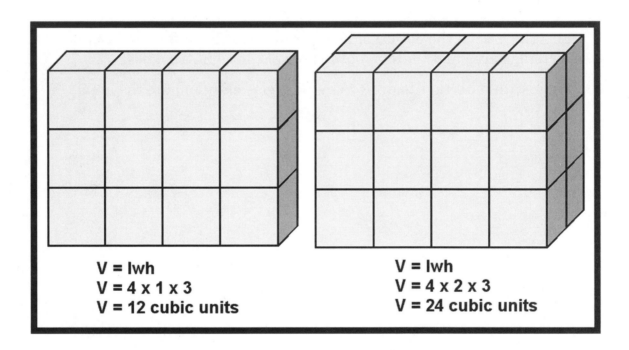

V = lwh
V = 4 x 1 x 3
V = 12 cubic units

V = lwh
V = 4 x 2 x 3
V = 24 cubic units

- The *volume of a solid* is the amount of space it occupies in cubic units.

- The *volume of a rectangular prism or cube* equals the length times the width times the height. The formula is $V = l \times w \times h$.

1. In Microsoft Word, go to View and choose Toolbars, then Drawing.

2. On the Drawing toolbar, choose AutoShapes, Basic Shapes, Cube.

3. Left click on the screen to insert the shape. You may use the upper right field handle to skew the cube (make it smaller). Wait for the double arrow to appear and hold down the left button on the mouse to skew.

*(continued)*

4. On the Drawing toolbar, choose the Fill Color button options to color your cube.

5. Go to Edit and choose Copy.

6. Open Paint.

7. Go to Edit and choose Paste.

8. Move the cube down the screen.

9. Paste another cube and move it to the right of the first cube.

10. Continue to paste and stack cubes from left to right until you have three rows of four cubes.

11. The rectangular prism you made has length, width, height, and area. Count the number of cubes in the stack. This is the volume of the stack and it is expressed in cubic units.

12. Click on the Select button and choose transparent from the section at the bottom of the Tool Box. Select the stack.

13. Go to Edit and choose Copy.

14. Go to Edit and choose Paste.

15. Move the pasted stack down the screen. Paste another stack in front of the original stack. What is the volume of the double stack? (Count the cubes, remembering to count the ones you don't see.) How does the number of cubes in the stacks compare to the relationship of the length, width, and height of the two stacks combined?

16. Click on the Text button and drag text boxes under the rectangular prisms. Type in the formula for the volume of a rectangular prism and the values for length, width, height, and volume.

17. Work with a partner to create other stacks and calculate the volume.

# Change for a Dollar

◆

*Objective:* To create and use representations to organize, record, and interpret a currency problem using the Paint Tool Box and Color Box

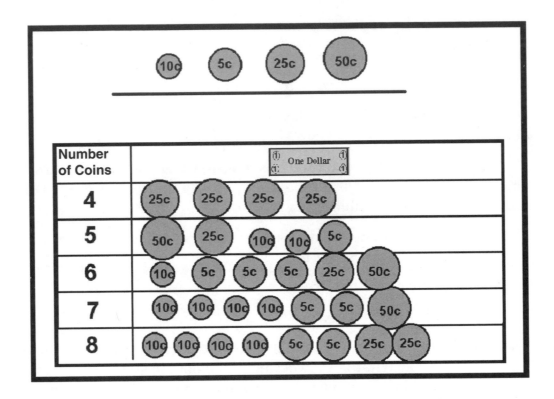

1. Click on the Line button and choose the second size from the section at the bottom of the Tool Box.

2. Right click on green and left click on black in the Color Box.

3. Click on the Rectangle button and choose opaque from the section at the bottom of the Tool Box. Drag a small green rectangle on the screen.

4. Click on the Text button and drag a small text box. On the Text Toolbar, choose Arial font, size 18, and bold. Type "One Dollar."

5. Click on the Select button and choose transparent from the section at the bottom of the Tool Box. Select the text and move it inside the dollar.

6. Right click on light gray in the Color Box.

*(continued)*

7. Click on the Ellipse button and choose opaque from the section at the bottom of the Tool Box. Drag (while holding down the Shift key) a small gray circle to represent a 50-cent coin.

8. Drag a smaller circle to represent a quarter.

9. Drag a smaller circle to represent a nickel.

10. Drag a smaller circle to represent a dime.

11. Right click on white in the Color Box.

12. Click on the Text button and drag a small text box. Type "5c," "10c," "25c," and "50c."

13. Click on the Select button and choose transparent from the section at the bottom of the Tool Box. Select and move the numbers inside the proper coins.

14. Click on the Rectangle button and choose transparent from the section at the bottom of the Tool Box. Drag a large rectangle.

15. Click on the Line button and choose the thinnest line from the section at the bottom of the Tool Box. Drag a vertical line down the table to make a column to the left. Draw horizontal lines across the table to make five rows that are evenly spaced.

16. Click on the Text button and drag a text box. At the top of the first column, type "Number of Coins."

17. Click on the Select button and choose transparent from the section at the bottom of the Tool Box. Select the dollar and move it to the top row, second column.

18. Click on the Text button and choose font size 20 from the Text Toolbar. Type the numbers 4, 5, 6, 7, and 8.

19. Click on the Select button and move the numbers to the first column of the table.

20. For each row, fill in the coins that you would need to make up a dollar using the number of coins indicated in the first column. Use the Select button and copy and paste, and move the pictures of these coins to the correct place in the second column.

21. Explain the strategy you used to your teacher or a classmate.

# Making Change

*Objective:* To develop an understanding of counting change using the Paint Tool Box and Color Box

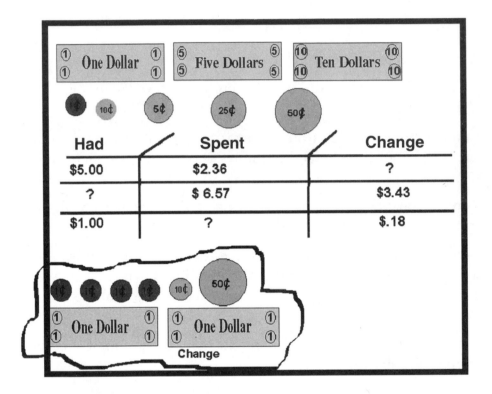

1. Click on the Rectangle button and choose transparent from the section at the bottom of the Tool Box. Drag a small rectangle in the shape of a dollar bill.

2. Click on the Select button and choose transparent from the section at the bottom of the Tool Box. Select the rectangle.

3. Go to Edit and choose Copy.

4. Go to Edit and choose Paste twice.

5. Click on the Text button and choose size 14 from the Text Toolbar. Type "One Dollar," "Five Dollars," and "Ten Dollars."

*(continued)*

6. Click on the Select button and select the text you want to move into each rectangle.

7. Click on the Fill With Color button and choose green from the Color Box. Color your bills green.

8. Click on the Ellipse button and choose transparent from the section at the bottom of the Tool Box. Choose black in the Color Box. Drag different-size circles (while holding down the Shift key) to represent a penny, a nickel, a quarter, and a half-dollar.

9. Click on the Fill With Color button to color the coins gray and brown.

10. Click on the Text button and choose Arial font, size 10, and bold from the Text Toolbar. Type "1c," "5c," "10c," "25c," and "50c."

11. Click on the Line button and drag a small line down the middle of each "c" to make the cent sign.

12. Click on the Select button and choose transparent from the section at the bottom of the Tool Box. Move each cent amount onto the appropriate coin.

13. Go to File and Save with the title "[Your Name]'s Money."

14. Either alone or with a partner, work out problems about making change. For example, what change would you receive from a five-dollar bill if you spent $2.36? To solve the problem, select and copy the coin pictures that you would need to make change. First, select the penny; copy and paste four to make $2.40. Then copy and paste the coins needed to reach $3.00. Finally, copy and paste the dollar bills needed to reach $5.00. Add up the change ($2.64). You may want to record your data on a data table. In the table, you can use the headings "Had," "Spent," and "Change."

15. Try solving problems when you're given the "Change" and the "Spent" amounts. How much was the "Had" amount?

16. Try solving problems when you're given the "Change" and the "Had" amounts. How much was the "Spent" amount?

17. When you close the document, do not save your changes.

# Constructing and Naming Angles

········································◆········································

*Objective:* To develop an understanding of naming angles according to their measures using the Paint Tool Box and Color Box.

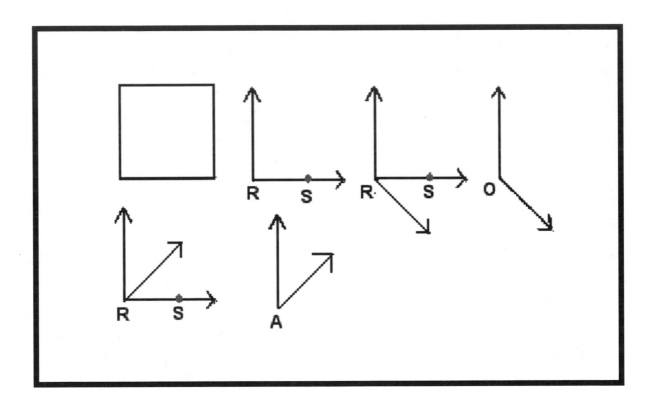

- A *right angle* measures 90 degrees.

- An *acute angle* measures less than 90 degrees.

- An *obtuse angle* measures more than 90 degrees.

**1.** Click on the Rectangle button and choose transparent from the section at the bottom of the Tool Box. Drag a rectangle.

*(continued)*

2. Click on the Select button and choose transparent from the section at the bottom of the Tool Box. Select the rectangle.

3. Go to Edit and choose Copy.

4. Go to Edit and choose Paste.

5. Click on the Eraser button. Erase the top right sides of the rectangle, saving the bottom left angle.

6. Click on the Line button. Drag lines to draw arrows at the ends of the sides.

7. Right and left click on red in the Color Box.

8. Click on the Ellipse button and choose opaque from the section at the bottom of the Tool Box. Drag a small point on the horizontal side of the angle.

9. Right click on white and left click on black in the Color Box.

10. Click on the Text button and drag small text boxes to name the angle "R" and the point "S." This forms the ray RS.

11. Angle R is a right angle (a 90-degree angle).

12. Click on the Select button and choose transparent from the section at the bottom of the Tool Box. Select the figure.

13. Go to Edit and choose Copy.

14. Go to Edit and choose Paste.

15. Move the pasted figure down on the screen.

16. Click on the Line button and drag a ray on the pasted figure starting at vertex R and going below ray RS.

17. Click on the Eraser button and erase ray RS from the second figure. Erase the R.

18. Click on the Text button and name the new angle "O."

19. Angle O is an obtuse angle (greater than 90 degrees).

20. Go to Edit and choose Paste.

*(continued)*

**21.** Click on the Line button and drag a line from vertex R above ray RS on the third figure.

**22.** Click on the Eraser button and erase RS from the third figure. Erase the R.

**23.** Click on the Text button and name the new angle "A."

**24.** Angle A is an acute angle (less than 90 degrees).

**25.** Click on the Text button and drag a text box in which to type the definitions of a right angle, an obtuse angle, and an acute angle.

# Sum of Angles in a Triangle and a Quadrilateral

· · · · · · · · · · · · · · · ◆ · · · · · · · · · · · · · · · ·

*Objective:* To investigate the sum of the angles of a triangle and a quadrilateral using the Paint Tool Box, menu bar, and Color Box

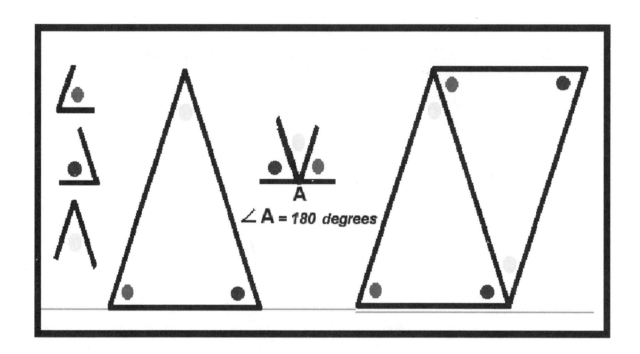

- A straight angle measures 180 degrees.

- The sum of the angles of a triangle equals 180 degrees.

- The sum of the angles of a quadrilateral equals 360 degrees.

1. Click on the Line button and choose the third line size from the section at the bottom of the Tool Box. Drag lines to draw a medium-size triangle.

2. Right click and left click on red in the Color Box.

3. Click on the Ellipse button and choose opaque from the section at the bottom of the Tool Box.

*(continued)*

**4.** Place the pointer inside the left base angle of the triangle and drag a small red circle.

**5.** Right click and left click on blue in the Color Box.

**6.** Place the pointer inside the right base angle and drag a small blue circle.

**7.** Right click and left click on yellow in the Color Box.

**8.** Place the pointer inside the top angle and drag a small yellow circle.

**9.** Right click on white in the Color Box.

**10.** Click on the Free-Form Select button and choose transparent from the section at the bottom of the Tool Box.

**11.** Click and drag a circle around the red angle.

**12.** Go to Edit and choose Copy.

**13.** Go to Edit and choose Paste.

**14.** Move the pasted angle down the screen.

**15.** Use the same procedure to copy and paste the yellow and the blue angles.

**16.** Click on the Select button and move the blue and red angles so that their vertices touch.

**17.** Select the yellow angle.

**18.** Go to Image and choose Flip/Rotate and Flip Vertical.

**19.** Move the yellow angle into the space between the red and blue angles. Do the angles form a straight angle?

**20.** Click on the Text button and drag a text box to label the straight angle, "$\angle A = 180$ degrees."

**21.** Try moving the blue and yellow angles so that their vertices touch and try moving the red angle into the space. Do they form a straight angle?

**22.** Click on the Select button and choose transparent from the section at the bottom of the Tool Box. Select the triangle.

**23.** Go to Edit and choose Copy.

**24.** Go to Edit and choose Paste.

*(continued)*

**25.** Go to Image and choose Flip/Rotate and Flip Vertical.

**26.** Move the flipped triangle and connect it to the original to form a quadrilateral. What do you conclude about the sum of the angles of this quadrilateral? (If the angles of a triangle add up to 180 degrees, then the two triangles together must add up to 360 degrees.)

**27.** Choose the Rectangle button to drag (while holding down the Shift key) a square.

**28.** Work with a partner to prove the sum of the angles is 360 degrees.

# Section 4

◆

# ALGEBRA

# Color Tile Patterns

Objective: To create color patterns using the Paint Tool Box and Color Box

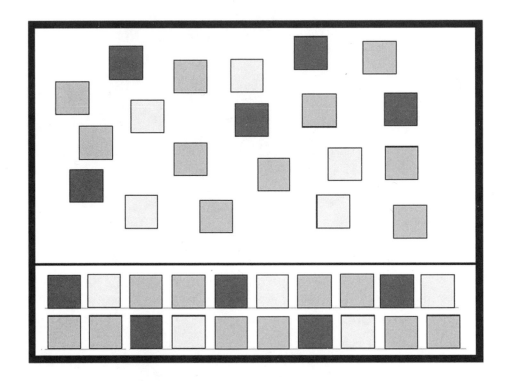

- *Patterns* are formed when something is copied or repeated.

1. Click on the Rectangle button and drag (while holding down the Shift key) a small square.

2. Click on the Select button and chose transparent from the section at the bottom of the Tool Box. Select the square.

3. Go to Edit and choose Copy.

4. Go to Edit and choose Paste.

5. Continue to paste until there are twenty squares. Move each square down to a different spot on the page after you paste it.

*(continued)*

**6.** Click on the Fill With Color button and color five squares red, five yellow, and ten green.

**7.** Click on the Select button and move the squares to create a pattern.

**8.** Click on the Text button and drag a text box under the pattern. Type "[Your Name]'s Pattern."

**9.** Work with a partner to create different patterns.

# Geometric Patterns

*Objective:* To represent and analyze geometric patterns using the Paint Tool Box and Color Box

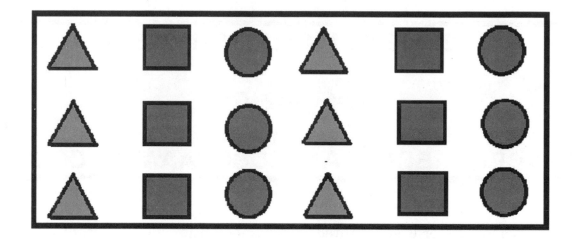

1. Click on the Line button and drag lines to draw a small triangle.

2. Click on the Rectangle button and drag a rectangle that is about the size of the triangle.

3. Click on the Ellipse button and drag a circle that is about the same size as the triangle and the rectangle.

4. Click on the Select button and move the triangle, rectangle, and circle side by side in a row.

5. Click on the Fill With Color button and color each shape a different color.

6. Click on the Select button and select all three shapes.

7. Go to Edit and choose Copy.

8. Go to Edit and choose Paste.

9. Move the pasted row to form a pattern.

10. Continue to paste until the pattern is repeated at least five times.

11. Use the Select button to make a different pattern.

# Changing Patterns

· · · · · · · · · · · · · · · · · · · ◆ · · · · · · · · · · · · · · · · · · · ·

*Objective:* To create patterns and introduce variables using the Microsoft Word Formatting toolbar

---

**122311223311122333111122 3333**

**A=1, B=2, C=3**

**ABBCAABBCCAAABBCCCAAAABBCCCC**

---

- When a letter is substituted for a number, it is called a *variable*.

1. In Microsoft Word, go to View and choose Toolbars, Formatting, and Standard.

2. On the Formatting toolbar, choose Arial font, size 20, and bold, and type this numeric pattern: 122311223311122333111122 3333.

3. Explain the pattern.

4. Type a capital letter for each number used in the pattern (for example, A = 1, B = 2, C = 3).

5. Click and drag over the letters to select them all at once. Go to the Formatting toolbar and change the color to red.

6. Type the pattern using the letters for the numbers they represent. What is the total value of the A's in your pattern? (10) What is the total value of the B's in your pattern? (16) What is the total value of the C's in your pattern? (30) Note that the number of A's and C's in the pattern is the same; however the value of C is three times the value of A. (Total value of A = 1 × 10 = 10, total value of C = 3 × 10 = 30.)

*(continued)*

7. Work with a partner to construct other numeric patterns using different numbers and change them to letter patterns.

8. Compute the values of the variables.

9. Type any observations from your patterns.

# Hundred Board Patterns

· · · · · · · · · · · · · · · · · · · ◆ · · · · · · · · · · · · · · · · · · ·

*Objective:* To represent and analyze patterns and functions on a hundred board using the Microsoft Word Tables and Borders toolbar

| 1 | 2 | 3 | 4 | 5 | 6 | 7 | 8 | 9 | 10 |
|---|---|---|---|---|---|---|---|---|---|
| 11 | 12 | 13 | 14 | 15 | 16 | 17 | 18 | 19 | 20 |
| 21 | 22 | 23 | 24 | 25 | 26 | 27 | 28 | 29 | 30 |
| 31 | 32 | 33 | 34 | 35 | 36 | 37 | 38 | 39 | 40 |
| 41 | 42 | 43 | 44 | 45 | 46 | 47 | 48 | 49 | 50 |
| 51 | 52 | 53 | 54 | 55 | 56 | 57 | 58 | 59 | 60 |
| 61 | 62 | 63 | 64 | 65 | 66 | 67 | 68 | 69 | 70 |
| 71 | 72 | 73 | 74 | 75 | 76 | 77 | 78 | 79 | 80 |
| 81 | 82 | 83 | 84 | 85 | 86 | 87 | 88 | 89 | 90 |
| 91 | 92 | 93 | 94 | 95 | 96 | 97 | 98 | 99 | 100 |

Copyright © 2005 by John Wiley & Sons, Inc.

- A *function* is a relationship between the elements of two sets. It can only produce one result.

- A *factor* of a number is a number that divides evenly into that number.

- If a number is a factor of another number, it is also a factor of the multiples of that number.

1. Open the "[Your Name]'s Hundred Board" document you created in the activity on page 56.

2. Go to Edit and choose Select All.

*(continued)*

3. Go to Edit and choose Copy.

4. Close the original document.

5. Go to File and choose New.

6. On the Formatting toolbar, choose Center Align.

7. Go to Edit and choose Paste.

8. Go to View on the menu bar and choose Toolbars, Tables and Borders.

9. On the Tables and Borders toolbar, choose the Shading Color button options and choose a color.

10. Click and drag over the number 6 in your table, then click on the Shading Color button on the Tables and Borders toolbar. The 6 cell is now shaded in the color that you chose.

11. Count up six cells and shade that cell.

12. Continue to shade every sixth cell. The shaded cells are multiples of 6. Do you see a pattern on the table?

13. Type the function for the shaded patterns that you see in each column. (+30) What are the next three numbers in the pattern following 96? (102, 108, 114) What numbers other than 1 are factors of all the multiples of 6? (2, 3)

14. Work with a partner to model other patterns.

15. Type any conclusions or functions that you discover in your patterns.

# Fun Patterns

Copyright © 2005 by John Wiley & Sons, Inc.

*Objective:* To generate patterns using the Paint Tool Box and Color Box and Microsoft Word AutoShapes

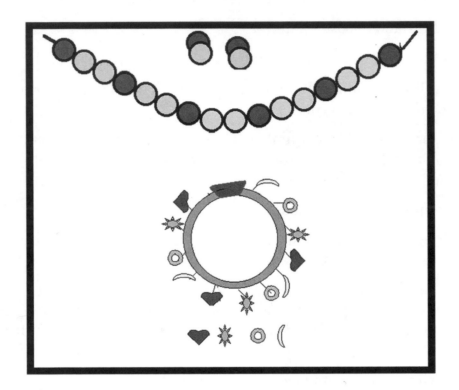

1.  In Paint, click on the Curve button and drag a line across the screen. Left click in the middle of the line and hold the mouse button down as you pull a curve in the line. Click again to set the curve. This will be a necklace.

2.  Click on the Ellipse button to drag a small circle. This will be a bead.

3.  Click on the Select button and choose transparent from the section at the bottom of the Tool Box. Select the bead.

4.  Go to Edit and choose Copy.

5.  Go to Edit and choose Paste.

*(continued)*

**6.** Move the pasted bead onto the necklace.

**7.** Continue to paste and move beads onto the necklace.

**8.** Click on the Fill With Color button and color the beads to form a pattern.

**9.** Paste more beads to make a pair of earrings to match the necklace.

**10.** Click on the Ellipse button and drag a circle. This will be a charm bracelet.

**11.** Open Microsoft Word, go to AutoShapes, and pick the charm shapes for the bracelet.

**12.** Left click on each charm and choose the Fill Color button on the Drawing toolbar to color the charms.

**13.** Left click on each charm, then go to Edit and choose Copy.

**14.** In the Paint window, go to Edit and choose Paste.

**15.** Continue to go from Microsoft Word to Paint until all the charms are pasted in Paint.

**16.** Click on the Select button in Paint to copy and move each charm to form a pattern of charms on the bracelet.

# Numeric Patterns

· · · · · · · · · · · · · · · · · · · · · ◆ · · · · · · · · · · · · · · · · · · · · ·

*Objective:* To represent and analyze numeric patterns and functions using the Paint Tool Box and Color Box

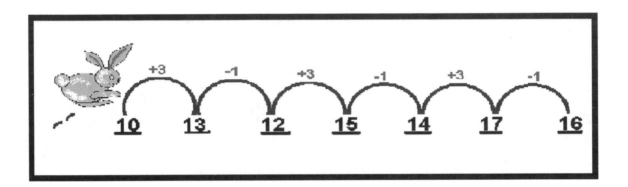

- *Number patterns* are formed when numerical operations are copied or repeated.

- The *tangent to a curve* is a straight line just touching the curve.

- An *arc* is part of a circle.

1. Click on the Line button and choose the third thickest line from the section at the bottom of the Tool Box.

2. Click on the Ellipse button and choose blue from the Color Box. Drag a medium-size circle.

3. Click on the Select button and choose transparent from the section at the bottom of the Tool Box. Select the circle. (Drag the select box so that the sides are tangent to [just touching] the circle.)

4. Go to Edit and choose Copy.

5. Go to Edit and choose Paste.

6. Move the pasted circle to the right of the original so that the circles touch evenly.

7. Continue to paste until there are six circles touching in a row.

*(continued)*

**8.** Click on the Select button and select the bottom halves of all the circles in the row.

**9.** Click on the Delete button on the keyboard. You should now have six arcs that are touching. The arcs will represent what happens in your number pattern.

**10.** Click on the Text button and drag a text box. Choose Arial font, size 16, and bold from the Text Toolbar and red from the Color Box. Type "+3" and "–1."

**11.** Click on the Select button and select the +3.

**12.** Go to Edit and choose Copy.

**13.** Go to Edit and choose Paste.

**14.** Move the pasted +3 over the first arc.

**15.** Continue to paste the +3 over the third and fifth arcs.

**16.** Click on the Select button and select the –1.

**17.** Copy and paste the –1 above the second, fourth, and sixth arcs.

**18.** Click on the Text button and drag a text box under the arcs.

**19.** Type a one- or two-digit number at the first end of the first arc.

**20.** Add 3 to that number and type that number at the end of the first arc. (Use the Select button to position numbers.)

**21.** Continue to follow the directions above the arcs and type in the resulting numbers at the ends of the arcs. You have created a number pattern.

**22.** Change the numbers above the arc to create new number patterns.

**23.** Work with a classmate to create and solve different patterns.

# Forming Patterns with Triangles

*Objective:* To describe, extend, and make generalizations about geometric patterns using the Microsoft Word Drawing toolbar and the Paint Tool Box and Color Box

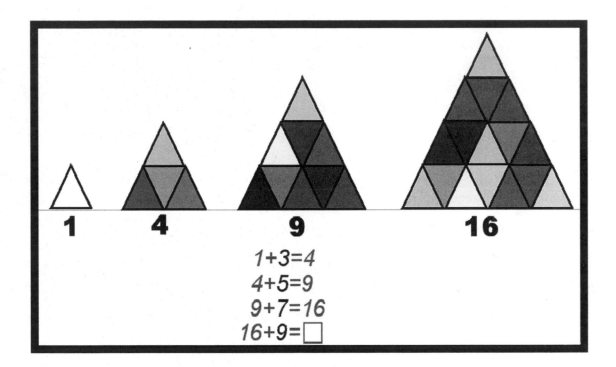

1. In Microsoft Word, go to View and choose Toolbars and Drawing.

2. On the Drawing toolbar, choose AutoShapes, Basic Shapes, and click on the Isosceles Triangle button.

3. Left click the mouse inside the document to insert the triangle.

4. On the Drawing toolbar, choose the Line Style button in $2\frac{1}{4}$ pt.

5. Go to Edit and choose Copy.

*(continued)*

6. Open Paint.

7. Go to Edit and choose Paste.

8. Move the pasted triangle down on the screen.

9. Place the pointer (wait for the double arrow to appear) on the upper right field handle to skew the triangle to a smaller size.

10. Go to Edit and choose Copy.

11. Go to Edit and choose Paste.

12. Move the pasted triangle down.

13. Paste another triangle and move it so that one of the base angles touches a base angle of the second triangle.

14. Paste another triangle and move it on top of the two touching triangles so that its base angles touch the tops of the other triangles. You have formed a larger triangle.

15. Paste three more triangles and line them up with their base angles touching.

16. Continue to paste and move triangles onto these three triangles until a large triangle is formed.

17. Paste four more triangles and line them up with their base angles touching. Build a large triangle in the same way as you did the other triangles.

18. Click on the Fill With Color button and color all the small triangles in different colors.

19. Count the number of small triangles in each large triangle.

20. Click on the Text button and drag a text box to record your results. (1, 4, 9, 16) Do you see a pattern? (Hint: Find the difference between each number and describe the numbers that are the differences [consecutive odd numbers].) How many small triangles would be in the next large triangle?

# Constructing Staircase Rods

*Objective:* To construct a computer manipulative for modeling math concepts using the Paint Tool Box and Color Box

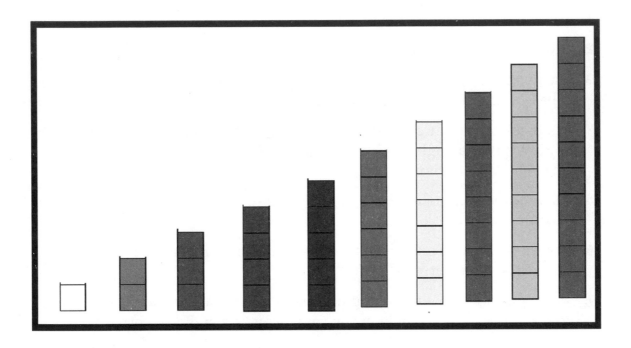

1. Click on the Line button and choose the thinnest line size from the section at the bottom of the Tool Box.

2. Click on the Rectangle button and choose transparent from the section at the bottom of the Tool Box. Drag a small square (while holding down the Shift key).

3. Click on the Select button and select the square.

4. Go to Edit and choose Copy.

5. Go to Edit and choose Paste.

*(continued)*

6. Move the pasted square down the screen. This will be your 1-unit rod. You will make rods that increase by 1 unit.

7. Go to Edit and choose Paste again. Move the pasted square on top of the other square to form a 2-unit rod.

8. Continue to select, copy, and paste until you have made unit rods representing 1 to 10 units. (Hint: Copy and paste eight more 1-unit rods, then copy and paste each previous rod. Use the Select button to move a 1-unit rod on top of the pasted copy of the previous rod.)

9. Click on the Fill With Color button and choose a different color from the Color Box to color each rod.

10. Save with the title "[Your Name]'s Staircase Rods."

# Staircase Rod Patterns

*Objective:* To generate, model, and interpret patterns using the Paint Tool Box and Color Box

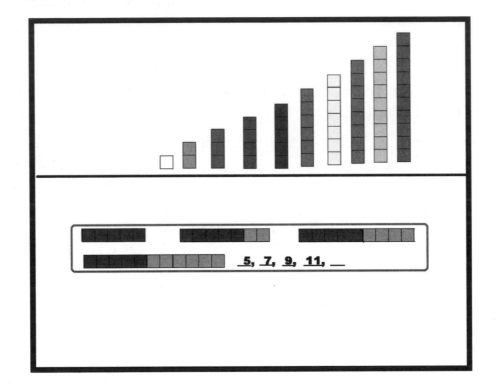

1. Open the document "[Your Name]'s Staircase Rods" that you created in the previous activity.

2. Click on the Select button and select the rods.

3. Go to Edit and choose Copy.

4. Close the original document.

5. Go to File and choose New.

6. Go to Edit and choose Paste.

7. Click on the Select button and choose transparent from the section at the bottom of the Tool Box. Select the 5-unit rod.

*(continued)*

8. Go to Edit and choose Copy.

9. Go to Edit and choose Paste.

10. Go to Image, Flip/Rotate, and choose Rotate by angle 90°.

11. Go to Edit and choose Copy.

12. Go to Edit and choose Paste to paste three more 5-unit rods.

13. Select the 2-unit rod and follow the same procedure to make a copy that is rotated 90 degrees.

14. Copy and paste five more rotated 2-unit rods.

15. Select and move the rods to form four sets: one 5-unit rod; one 2-unit rod on a 5-unit rod; two 2-unit rods on a 5-unit rod; and three 2-unit rods on a 5-unit rod.

16. Click on the Text button and drag a text box. Type the sums for each set. Do see a number pattern?

17. Work with a partner to build other rod patterns and type their number patterns.

# Area and Perimeter

. . . . . . . . . . . . . . . . . . . . . . ◆ . . . . . . . . . . . . . . . . . . . . .

*Objective:* To identify and model formulas for area and perimeter using the Paint Tool Box and Color Box

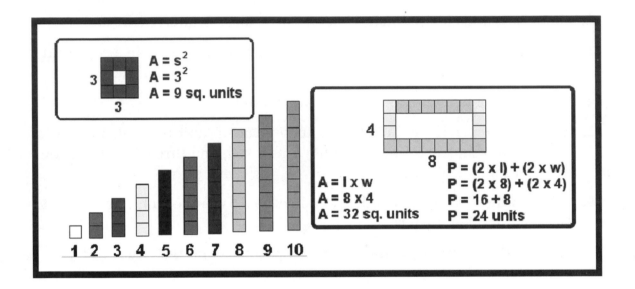

1. Open the document "[Your Name]'s Staircase Rods" that you created in the activity on page 140.

2. Click on the Select button and select the rods.

3. Go to Edit and choose Copy.

4. Go to File and choose New.

5. Go to File and choose Paste. You are going to make a rectangle using the rods to represent the sides.

6. Click on the Select button and select a rod for the length of your rectangle.

7. Go to Edit and choose Copy.

8. Go to Edit and chose Paste.

9. Go to Image, Flip/Rotate, and choose Rotate angle by 90°.

*(continued)*

10. Go to Edit and choose Copy.

11. Go to Edit and choose Paste.

12. Click on the Select button and select a rod for the width of your rectangle.

13. Go to Edit and choose Copy.

14. Go to Edit and choose Paste.

15. Select the rods and move them to form a rectangle (the rods will overlap at the corners).

16. Click on the Text button and drag a text box. Type the formulas for the area and the perimeter of a rectangle.

17. Substitute the rod values you used for length and width in the formulas. A square is a rectangle that has four equal sides. Can you think of a special formula for the area of a square? Can you prove the area using the 1-unit rod?

18. Work with a partner to model other rectangles and find their areas and perimeters.

# Constructing Fraction Rods

*Objective:* To represent equations of commonly used fractions using the Microsoft Word Ruler and Drawing toolbar and the Paint Tool Box and Color Box

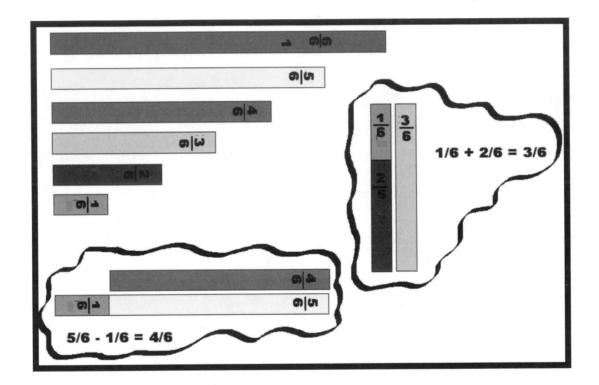

1. In Microsoft Word, choose View, Toolbars, Drawing, and Ruler.

2. On the Drawing toolbar, choose Rectangle and click inside the screen to insert the rectangle.

3. Move the rectangle up near the beginning of the ruler for measuring.

4. Place the pointer on the right-side field handle and stretch the rectangle to form a 6-inch rod.

5. Click on the 6-inch rod and hold down the left mouse button as you move the rod down the screen.

*(continued)*

6. Go to Edit and choose Copy to copy the 6-inch rod.

7. Go to Edit and choose Paste.

8. Move the pasted rectangle near the ruler, and with the right-side field handle, skew the rectangle to form a 5-inch rod.

9. Continue to paste and skew rectangles to make a 4-inch, a 3-inch, a 2-inch, and a 1-inch rod.

10. Left click on each rod and choose a color from the Fill Color choices on the Drawing toolbar.

11. Go to Edit and choose Select All.

12. Go to Edit and choose Copy.

13. Open Paint.

14. Go to Edit and choose Paste.

15. Go to Image and choose Flip/Rotate by angle 90°.

16. Click on the Text button and drag a text box. Type "$\frac{6}{6}$," 1, "$\frac{5}{6}$," "$\frac{4}{6}$," "$\frac{3}{6}$," "$\frac{2}{6}$," and "$\frac{1}{6}$."

17. Click on the Select button and move each fraction to the appropriate rod (and the 1 to the $\frac{6}{6}$ rod).

18. Copy and paste rods to show that $\frac{1}{6} + \frac{2}{6} = \frac{3}{6}$.

19. Copy and paste rods to show that $\frac{5}{6} - \frac{1}{6} = \frac{4}{6}$.

20. Work with a partner to model more equations from the fraction rods.

# Distributive Property of Multiplication

*Objective:* To model the distributive property of multiplication using the Paint Tool Box and Color Box

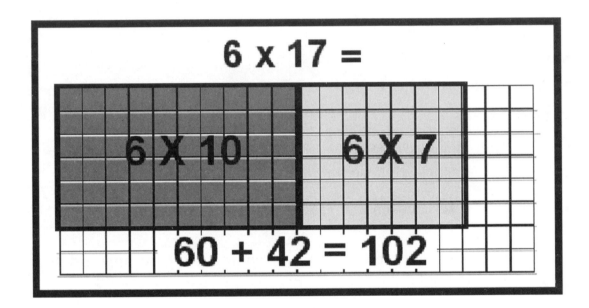

- Multiplication has a distributive property over addition. A distributive property is a property that relates two operations on numbers as multiplication and addition. This property gets its name because it "distributes" the factor outside the parentheses over the two terms within the parentheses.

1. Open the "[Your Name]'s 10 × 10 Grid" document that you created on page 78.

2. Go to Edit and choose Select All.

3. Go to Edit and choose Copy.

4. Close the original document.

*(continued)*

Copyright © 2005 by John Wiley & Sons, Inc.

5. Open Paint.

6. Go to Edit and choose Paste.

7. Choose the Select button to connect two grids.

8. The problem $6 \times 17$ can be solved on the grids using the distributive property $(6 \times 10) + (6 \times 7)$.

9. Click on the Fill With Color button and pick any color. Color in a $10 \times 6$ section of one grid.

10. Choose a different color and color in a $6 \times 7$ section of another grid.

11. Compute the answer using the distributive property $10 \times 6 = 60$ and $7 \times 6 = 42$, $60 + 42 = 102$. Compare the results to the total number of squares colored on the grids.

12. Model another problem in the form 1 digit $\times$ 2 digits.

13. Go to Image and choose Clear Image.

14. Go to Edit and choose Paste. Paste and connect enough grids to model the problem.

# Associative Property of Multiplication

· · · · · · · · · · · · · · · · · · · · · · · · · ◆ · · · · · · · · · · · · · · · · · · · · · · · · ·

*Objective:* To model the associative property of multiplication using the Paint Tool Box and Color Box

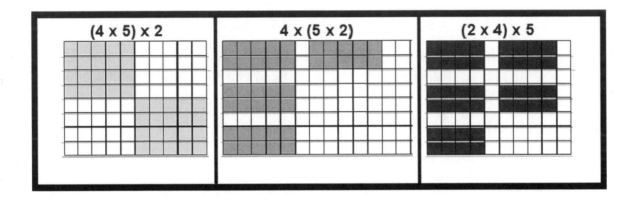

| (4 × 5) × 2 | 4 × (5 × 2) | (2 × 4) × 5 |

- The operation of multiplication is associative because the order of the combined elements does not change the product.

1. Open the "[Your Name]'s 10 × 10 Grid" document that you created on page 78.

2. Go to Edit and choose Select All.

3. Go to Edit and choose Copy.

4. Close the original document.

5. Open Paint.

6. Go to Edit and choose Paste.

7. Click on the Text button and drag a text box. Type "(4 × 5) × 2," "4 × (5 × 2)," and "(2 × 4) × 5."

8. First multiply the numbers in the parentheses, then multiply the product by the third number. What is the product for each set?

*(continued)*

9. Click on the Fill With Color button and color two $4 \times 5$ grids. This models $(4 \times 5) \times 2$.

10. Paste more grids to model $4 \times (5 \times 2)$ and $(2 \times 4) \times 5$.

11. Work with a partner to type and model other representations of the associative property of multiplication.

# Representing Variables

◆

*Objective:* To model problem situations with objects and to identify and compare various quantities using the Microsoft Word Drawing toolbar and the Paint Tool Box and Color Box

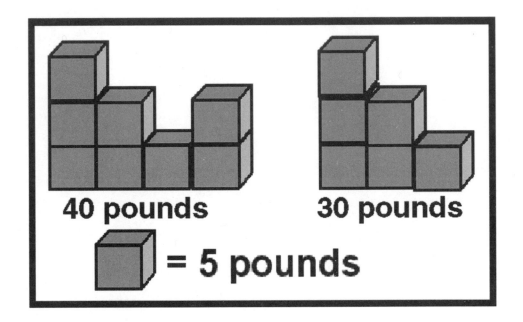

40 pounds      30 pounds

= 5 pounds

1. In Microsoft Word, go to View, Toolbars, and choose Drawing.

2. On the Drawing toolbar, go to AutoShapes, Basic Shapes, and choose Cube.

3. Place the pointer inside the document and left click the mouse to insert a cube.

4. On the Drawing toolbar, go to Line Style and choose $2\frac{1}{4}$ pt.

5. Go to Edit and choose Copy.

6. Open Paint.

7. Go to Edit and choose Paste.

8. Move the pasted cube down on the screen.

*(continued)*

9. Click on the Fill With Color button and choose orange from the Color Box. Click inside the cube to color it orange.

10. Click on the Select button and choose transparent from the section at the bottom of the Tool Box. Select the cube.

11. Go to Edit and choose Copy.

12. Go to Edit and choose Paste.

13. Continue to paste and move the cubes to form a picture of stacked boxes.

14. Paste a cube below the stacks. Click on the Text button and drag a text box next to this cube. Type "= 5 pounds" in the text box.

15. If each box weighs 5 pounds, what is the total weight of your stack?

16. Make a new stack of boxes and assign a new weight for the boxes.

17. Click on the Text button and drag a text box under each stack. Type the total weight of the stack.

18. Work with a classmate to ask and answer questions about your stacks.

# Magic Squares

◆

*Objective:* To develop an understanding of how a variable can be used in an algebraic expression using the Paint Tool Box and Color Box

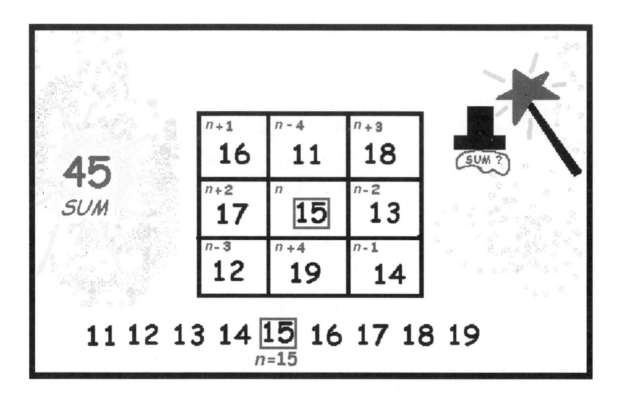

- A "magic square" is formed when the sum of the numbers in each column, row, and diagonal of a table is the same.

- *Consecutive* numbers are numbers that are in counting order.

- The *median* is the number in the middle of a set of consecutive numbers.

- *Variables* are letters or symbols used to represent numbers.

1. Click on the Rectangle button and choose transparent from the section at the bottom of the Tool Box. Drag a medium-size square.

*(continued)*

**2.** Click on the Line button and drag four lines that divide the square into nine equal-size smaller squares.

**3.** Click on the Text button and drag a text box. Choose font size 20 from the Text Toolbar and type nine consecutive numbers. The fifth number in the set is the median (the number in the middle).

**4.** Click on the Rectangle button and drag a frame around the median number in your list. This number will be equal to $n$ (a variable).

**5.** Click on the Text button, drag a text box, and choose red from the Color Box. Type an equation about $n$ ($n = 15$).

**6.** Drag another text box and choose font size 14. Type "$n$" and the following algebraic expressions: $n + 1$, $n - 1$, $n + 2$, $n - 2$, $n + 3$, $n - 3$, $n + 4$, $n - 4$.

**7.** Click on the Select button and choose transparent from the section at the bottom of the Tool Box. Move $n$ to the upper left-hand corner of the middle square.

**8.** Move the algebraic expressions as follows: $n + 1$ to the same position in the upper left square; $n - 1$ to the lower right square; $n + 2$ to the left middle square; $n - 2$ to the right middle square; $n + 3$ to the top right square; $n - 3$ to the bottom left square; $n + 4$ to the bottom middle square; and $n - 4$ to the top middle square.

**9.** Substitute 15 for $n$ in each expression and find the value in your set of numbers.

**10.** Select and move each number in your set to its proper place on the magic square. Are the sums of the numbers in each column, row, and diagonal the same? If so, then you have made a magic square.

**11.** Use your set of numbers to make a puzzle for a classmate.

**12.** List some of the properties you noticed in making the magic square.

# Algebraic Expressions

· · · · · · · · · · · · · · · · · · · · ◆ · · · · · · · · · · · · · · · · · · · ·

*Objective:* To generate, model, and interpret algebraic expressions using the Paint Tool Box and Color Box

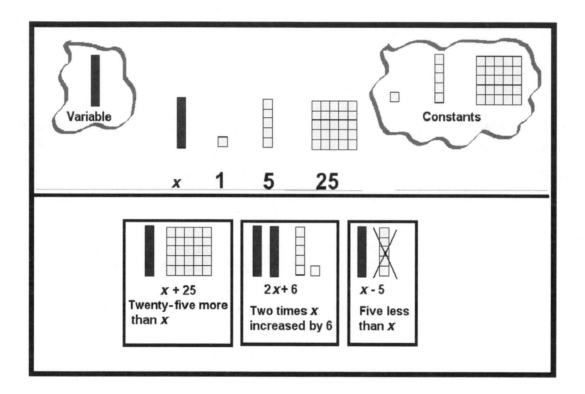

- A *constant* is a number whose value does not change.

1. In the Color Box, left click on black and right click on blue.

2. Click on the Rectangle button and choose opaque from the section at the bottom of the Tool Box. Drag a small blue rod shape. (This will represent the variable block.)

3. In the Color Box, right click on yellow.

4. Drag (while holding down the Shift key) a small yellow square. (This will represent the constant 1-unit block.)

*(continued)*

5. Click on the Select button and select the constant.

6. Go to Edit and choose Copy.

7. Go to Edit and choose Paste.

8. Continue to paste squares and connect them to form a yellow rod made of five squares. (This will represent the constant 5-unit block.)

9. Click on the Select button to select the yellow 5-unit block.

10. Go to Edit and choose Copy.

11. Go to Edit and choose Paste.

12. Continue to paste and connect the rods to form a $5 \times 5$ square block. (This will represent the constant 25-unit block.)

13. Use Select, Copy, and Paste to model the algebraic expression $x + 25$.

14. Click on the Text button and drag a text box. Type word expressions that may be represented with $x + 25$ (for example, "25 more than $x$," "$x$ increased by 25").

15. Use Select, Copy, and Paste to model the algebraic expression $x - 5$. (Click on the Line button and drag lines to cross out the constant 5-unit block.)

16. Work with a partner to model more algebraic expressions and word expressions.

# Solving Simple Equations

•  •  •  •  •  •  •  •  •  •  •  •  •  •  ◆  •  •  •  •  •  •  •  •  •  •  •  •  •  •

*Objective:* To model and solve simple algebraic equations using the Paint Tool Box and Color Box

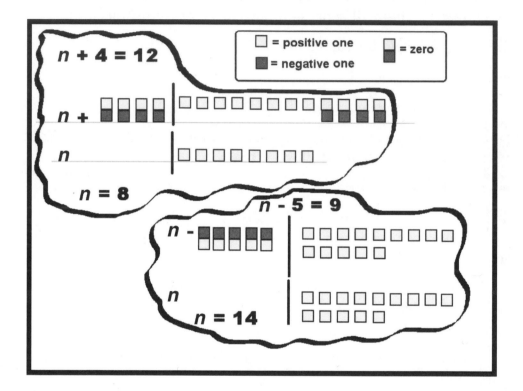

1. Click on the Line button and choose the thinnest line size from the section at the bottom of the Tool Box.

2. Right click on yellow and left click on black in the Color Box.

3. Click on the Rectangle button and drag (while holding down the Shift key) a small yellow square with a black line border. This will represent positive one. Type "= positive one" to the right of the square.

4. Click on the Select button and choose transparent from the section at the bottom of the Tool Box. Select the square.

5. Go to Edit and choose Copy.

*(continued)*

**6.** Go to Edit and choose Paste.

**7.** Move the pasted square down on the screen.

**8.** Click on the Fill With Color button and choose red from the Color Box. Color the pasted square red. This will represent negative one. Type "= negative one" to the right of the square.

**9.** Copy and paste one yellow square and one red square. Put them together to represent zero. Type "= zero" to the right of the squares.

**10.** You will model solving for $n$ in the equation $n + 4 = 12$.

**11.** Click on the Line button and drag a vertical line on the screen. This will represent the equal sign.

**12.** Click on the Select button and select the positive one (yellow) square.

**13.** Go to Edit and choose Copy.

**14.** Go to Edit and choose Paste.

**15.** Move the pasted square down to the left of the equal line.

**16.** Paste three more positive squares next to it for a total of four.

**17.** Click on the Text button and drag a text box to on the left side of the four positive squares. Type "$n +$."

**18.** Click on the Select button and select the four positive squares.

**19.** Go to Edit and choose Copy.

**20.** Go to Edit and choose Paste.

**21.** Move the pasted squares to the right of the equal sign.

**22.** Continue to paste until there are twelve positive squares on the right side of the equal sign.

**23.** To make the equation read "$n$ equals," you must eliminate four from each side of the equation.

*(continued)*

## Solving Simple Equations *(continued)*

**24.** One negative added to one positive makes zero. Therefore, Select, Copy, and Paste four negatives on each side of the equation, connecting each to a positive (this will make four zeros on each side).

**25.** Select the four zeros on each side and use Delete on the keyboard to delete them.

**26.** Now count the remaining yellow squares and read the equation. You have solved for $n$ ($n = 8$).

**27.** Try using the same method to model the equation $n - 5 = 9$. The red squares will represent subtracting positive 5. What do you need to add to both sides to get "$n =$" (5)? What will $n$ equal? ($n = 14$).

**28.** Work with a partner to model other equations.

# Squaring a Number

*Objective:* To represent the idea of substituting value to a squared variable using the Paint Tool Box and Color Box

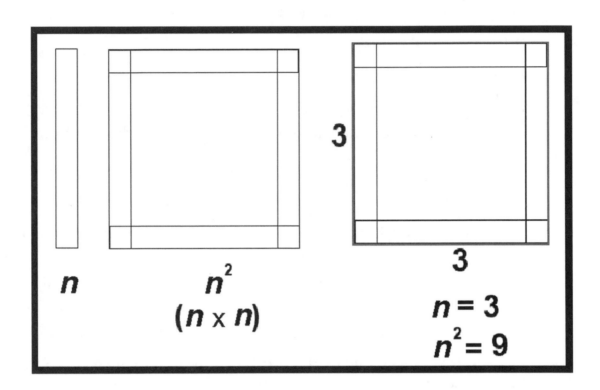

1. Click on the Line button and choose the thinnest line from the section at the bottom of the Tool Box.

2. Click on the Rectangle button and drag a tall skinny rectangle (rod). This rod will represent the variable $n$.

3. Click on the Select button and choose transparent from the section at the bottom of the Tool Box. Select the rectangle.

4. Go to Edit and choose Copy.

5. Go to Edit and Choose Paste.

6. Move the rectangle (rod) down on the screen.

*(continued)*

7. Go to Edit and choose Paste.

8. Go to Image and choose Flip/Rotate. In the message box, choose Flip Horizontal.

9. Move the horizontal rod to the bottom of the vertical rod so that their corners overlap (you will see a small square).

10. Select the L-shaped figure.

11. Go to Edit and choose Copy.

12. Go to Edit and choose Paste.

13. Go to Image and choose Flip/Rotate. In the message box, choose Flip Horizontal.

14. Go to Image again and choose Flip/Rotate. In the message box, choose Flip Vertical.

15. Move the upside-down L image to connect to the other L image to form a square (you will see a small square in each corner).

16. The area of this square is $n \times n$ (length $\times$ width) or $n^2$. Use the text button to label the box $n^2$.

17. Substitute a value of 3 for the variable $n$. The value of $n$ squared is 9.

18. Click on the Text button and drag a text box. Type other values of $n$ and compute the squares.

# Charting Variables

*Objective:* To investigate how a change in one variable relates to a change in a second variable using the Microsoft Word Tables and Borders toolbar and the Microsoft Excel Chart Wizard

$$y = x + 6$$

| x = | y = |
|:---:|:---:|
| 0 | 6 |
| 1 | 7 |
| 3 | 9 |
| 5 | 11 |
| 7 | 13 |
| 9 | 15 |
| 11 | 17 |
| 13 | 19 |

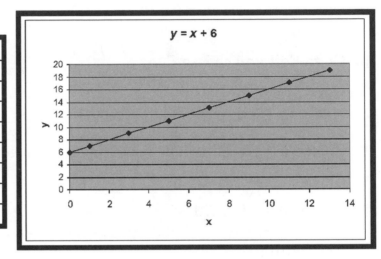

1. In Microsoft Word, type the equation $y = x + 6$.

2. Go to View, Toolbars, and choose Tables and Borders.

3. On the Tables and Borders toolbar, choose Insert Table.

4. In the message box, type 2 for the number of columns and 8 for the number of rows.

5. Beginning in the first cell, left click and drag to select the entire table.

6. On the Format bar, choose font size 22, bold, and center align.

7. Type "$x =$" in the first cell of the table.

8. Press the Tab key on the keyboard and type "$y =$" in the next cell in the first row.

9. Press the Tab key and type "0" in the first cell under "$x =$."

*(continued)*

**10.** Press the Down Arrow key on the keyboard and type "1."

**11.** Continue to press the Down Arrow key after typing each number in the first column: 3, 5, 7, 9, 11, and 13.

**12.** Substitute each value for $x$ to solve for $y$.

**13.** Type the values for $y$ in the second column. What patterns do you see in the table? How does $y$ relate to $x$?

**14.** Click on the cell with 0 and drag the mouse to select all the numbers on the table.

**15.** Go to Edit and choose Copy.

**16.** Open Microsoft Excel.

**17.** Go to Edit and choose Paste.

**18.** Click on the 0 cell and drag the mouse to select all the numbers.

**19.** Choose Insert, then Chart.

**20.** In the Chart Wizard Step 1, choose Chart type: XY (Scatter) and Chart sub-type: Scatter with data points connected by lines, then click on the Next button.

**21.** In the Chart Wizard Step 2, choose the Next button. In Step 3, type "$y = x + 6$" in the Chart title box, "$x$" in the Value (X) axis box, and "$y$" in the Value (Y) axis box, then click on the Next button. In Step 4, choose "As new sheet" and click on Finish. How does the line run? Why?

**22.** Work with a partner to create an equation with two variables and investigate how a change in one variable relates to a change in the other variable.

# Section 5

GEOMETRY

# Locating Points

*Objective:* To make and use coordinate systems to describe points using the Paint Tool Box and Color Box

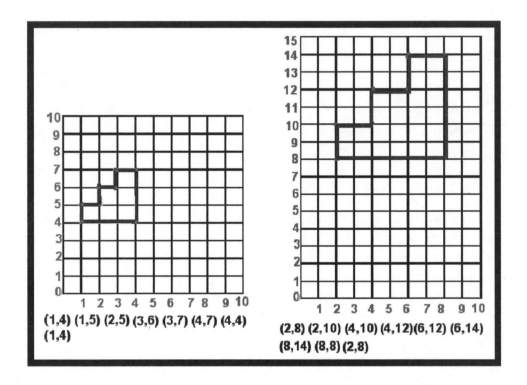

(1,4) (1,5) (2,5) (3,6) (3,7) (4,7) (4,4) (1,4)

(2,8) (2,10) (4,10) (4,12)(6,12) (6,14) (8,14) (8,8) (2,8)

- A pair of numbers that describe a point's position with reference to the *x*- and *y*- axes is a *coordinate*.

1. Open the document "[Your Name]'s 10 × 10 Grid" that you created in the activity on page 78.

2. Click on the Select button and choose transparent from the section at the bottom of the Tool Box. Select a grid.

3. Go to Edit and choose Copy.

4. Close the original document.

5. Go to File and choose New.

6. Go to Edit and choose Paste.

*(continued)*

7. Move the pasted grid down on the screen.

8. Click on the Text button and drag a text box. Type the numbers 0 through 10 and 1 through 10, leaving two spaces between each number. On the Text Toolbar, choose font size 12 and bold, and choose red from the Color Box.

9. Click on the Select button to move the 0 to a position on the outside of the grid at the lower left corner.

10. Move the rest of the numbers to their proper places outside the grid. They should increase from zero as they go up the left-hand side (the $y$-axis) and increase from zero as they go right on the bottom line (the $x$-axis).

11. Select the entire numbered grid.

12. Go to Edit and choose Copy.

13. Click on the Line button and choose the thickest size from the section at the bottom of the Tool Box. Choose any color from the Color Box and draw a polygon on the grid so that the vertices of the polygon are at points where $x$ intersects $y$. Using the Line button and red from the Color Box, click a dot on each vertex of the polygon.

14. Click on the Text button and drag a text box. Choose black from the Color Box. Type the coordinates of the polygon vertices in parentheses in this form $(x,y)$. Pick a starting point and move to the next vertex along a side, continuing until you are back to the starting point.

15. Work with a partner to check your coordinates.

16. Now multiply each pair of coordinates by 2. What do you predict the shape will be with the new coordinates? Will it be similar to or congruent to the original?

17. Click on the Line button and choose red from the Color Box to plot the points of the new coordinates on a new grid. (Go to Edit and paste a new grid if necessary.)

18. Choose another color from the Color Box and drag the lines to connect the points.

19. Click on the Text button and drag a text box. Type any observations and conclusions.

# Naming Triangles

◆

*Objective:* To classify triangles according to their properties using the Paint Tool Box and Color Box

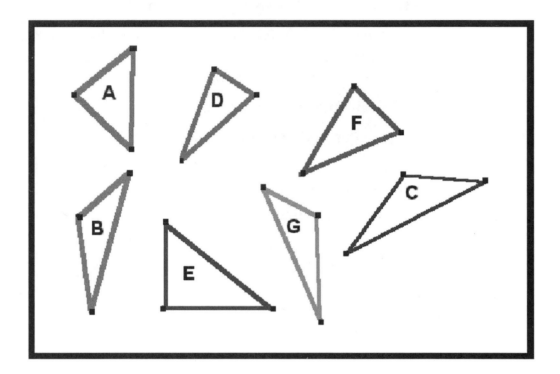

- A *triangle* is a polygon made with three straight sides.

- An *isosceles triangle* has two equal sides and two equal angles.

- An *equilateral triangle* has all three sides equal and all three angles equal.

- A *right triangle* has a right angle.

- A *scalene triangle* has no equal sides.

**1.** Click on the Text button and drag a text box. Type the definitions of the triangle types listed above.

**2.** Click on the Eraser button.

*(continued)*

**3.** Left click on black in the Color Box, then right click on black.

**4.** Place the pointer on the screen and click once to make a square dot. Click two more times to make a total of three dots that are not connected.

**5.** Click on the Line button and choose the fourth thickness from the section at the bottom of the Tool Box. Choose any color from the Color Box.

**6.** Choose the Polygon button and choose transparent from the section at the bottom of the Tool Box. Drag a line connecting two dots and left click on the other dot (a connecting line will appear).

**7.** Close the triangle by clicking on the starting dot.

**8.** Draw at least six triangles in this manner using different colors.

**9.** Click on the Text button and drag a text box. Type six uppercase letters and use them to label each triangle.

**10.** Work with a partner to choose the best name for each triangle from the list of definitions.

**11.** Click on the Text button and drag a text box. Type your conclusions.

# Constructing Polygons

*Objective:* To identify, compare, and analyze attributes of polygons and develop vocabulary to describe the attributes using the Paint Tool Box and Color Box

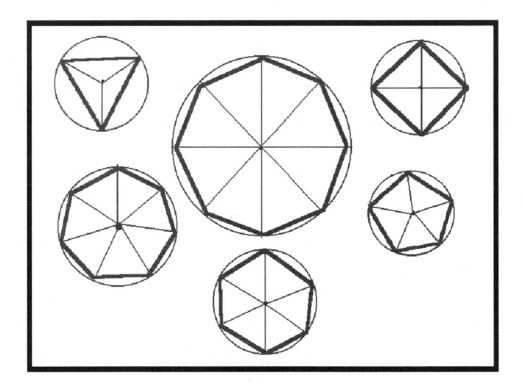

- A *polygon* is a plane shape bounded by only straight lines.
- A *triangle* is a polygon with three straight sides.
- A *quadrilateral* is a polygon with four straight sides.
- A *pentagon* is a polygon with five straight sides.
- A *hexagon* is a polygon with six straight sides.
- A *heptagon* is a polygon with seven straight sides.
- An *octagon* is a polygon with eight straight sides.

*(continued)*

- The *radius* of a circle is the distance from the center of the circle to a point on the circle. *Radii* is the plural of radius.

- A *sector* of a circle is a shape that includes an arc of the circle and two radii of the circle.

1. Click on the Line button and choose the thinnest line size from the section at the bottom of the Tool Box. Choose light gray from the Color Box.

2. Click on the Ellipse button and drag (while holding down the Shift key) a medium-size circle.

3. Click on the Line button and choose the thickest line from the section at the bottom of the Tool Box. Choose black from the Color Box.

4. Mark the center of the circle by making a quick left click. In the same way, mark three points on the circle that are the same distance apart. (Imagine you are dividing the circle into thirds.)

5. Choose the thinnest line in light gray to drag a line from the center to each point on the circle (making three radii). The circle is now divided into three sectors.

6. Select the thickest line and change the color to red.

7. Click on the Polygon button and drag a line from one point where the radius touches the circle to another point where the radius touches the circle. Then click on the next point and a line will automatically connect the two points.

8. Click again on the first point and a triangle will appear. How many equal sides does the triangle have? How many angles are in the triangle and what type are they? Are the sides of the triangle radii, chords, or diameters?

9. Construct other polygons by dividing circles into four, five, six, seven, and eight equal parts. This will determine the type of polygon.

10. Click on the Text button and drag a text box. Type the names and properties of the different polygons you constructed.

# Lines of Symmetry in a Rectangle and a Square

◆

*Objective:* To recognize and compare the number of lines of symmetry in a square and a rectangle using the Paint Tool Box and Color Box

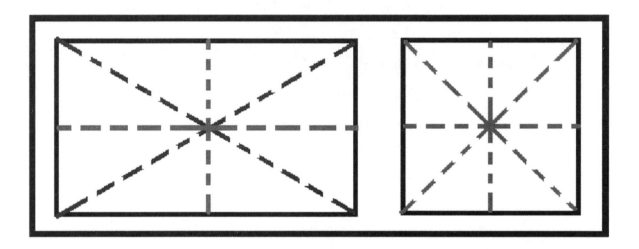

- *Symmetry* is the correspondence of parts on either side of a median line or plane of a shape.

- A *line of symmetry* is an imaginary line dividing a shape in such a way that half of the shape covers the other half exactly.

**1.** Click on the Line button and choose the thickest line size from the section at the bottom of the Tool Box.

**2.** Click on the Rectangle button and choose transparent from the section at the bottom of the Tool Box. Drag a large rectangle.

**3.** Click on the Line button and choose blue from the Color Box. Drag two diagonals on the rectangle, dividing the rectangle into two pairs of congruent triangles.

*(continued)*

**4.** Click on the Eraser button and do quick clicks along the lines to make dotted lines.

**5.** Left click on red in the Color Box.

**6.** Click on the Line button and drag (while holding down the Shift key) a vertical line connecting the top and bottom and passing through the point of intersection of the diagonals.

**7.** Connect the sides in the same way with a red horizontal line.

**8.** Click on the Eraser button and make dotted lines out of the red lines.

**9.** Go to File and choose Print.

**10.** Go to File and choose New.

**11.** In the message box, answer No to "Save changes to untitled?"

**12.** Click on the Rectangle button and drag (while holding down the Shift key) a large square.

**13.** Click on the Line button and choose red from the Color Box. Draw two red diagonal lines.

**14.** Draw horizontal, vertical, and diagonal lines as in the rectangle to divide the square into eight equal parts.

**15.** Click on the Eraser button and make all the red lines dotted lines.

**16.** Go to File and choose Print.

**17.** Cut out the rectangle and the square.

**18.** Make a fold on each red line and determine if it is a line of symmetry. Are the blue lines symmetry lines? How many lines of symmetry are in a rectangle? How many lines of symmetry are in a square?

# The ABCs of Symmetry

....................◆....................

*Objective:* To develop an understanding of symmetry and to recognize lines of symmetry using the Paint Tool Box and Color Box

1. Click on the Text button and drag a large text box.

2. Go to View and choose the Text Toolbar.

3. On the Text Toolbar, choose Arial font, size 48, and bold.

4. Choose black from the Color Box.

5. Type the letters of the alphabet in uppercase with one space between each letter.

6. Click on the Line button and choose the thickest line size from the section at the bottom of the Tool Box. Drag red lines of symmetry where you see them on the letters.

7. Choose blue from the Color Box and drag a blue X on letters that do not have a line of symmetry.

8. The letter O has an infinite number of lines of symmetry.

9. Go to File and choose Print so that you can compare and discuss your lines of symmetry with those of a classmate.

# Congruent and Similar

◆

*Objective:* To explore congruence and similarity using the Paint Tool Box and Color Box

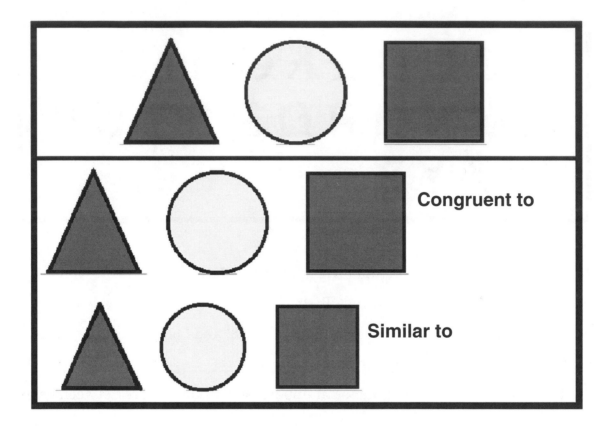

- *Congruent* means the same size and the same shape.
- *Similar* means the same shape but not the same size.

1. Click on the Line button and choose the third line size from the section at the bottom of the Tool Box. Draw a triangle.

2. Click on the Fill With Color button and choose any color from the Color Box. Color the triangle.

3. Left click on black and right click on yellow in the Color Box.

*(continued)*

4. Click on the Ellipse button and choose opaque from the section at the bottom of the Tool Box. Drag (while holding down the Shift key) a yellow circle with a black outline.

5. Right click on blue in the Color Box.

6. Click on the Rectangle button and choose opaque from the section at the bottom of the Tool Box. Drag (while holding down the Shift key) a blue rectangle or a square outlined in black.

7. Click on the Select button to move the shapes in a row.

8. Click on the Line button and drag (while holding down the Shift key) a line under the row of shapes.

9. Click on the Select button and select the three shapes.

10. Go to Edit and choose Copy.

11. Go to Edit choose Paste.

12. Move the pasted row of shapes under the original row. The pasted row has shapes that are congruent (same size and same shape) to the original shapes.

13. Go to Edit and choose Paste.

14. Move the pasted row under the other rows.

15. Place the pointer at the upper left field handle to skew or stretch the shapes. This row has shapes that are similar (same shape but not the same size) to the original shapes.

16. Click on the Text button and drag a text box to explain the terms *congruent* and *similar*.

# Fun with Shapes

*Objective:* To develop skills in identifying two- and three-dimensional shapes and spelling their names using the Microsoft Word menu bar and the Drawing and Standard toolbars

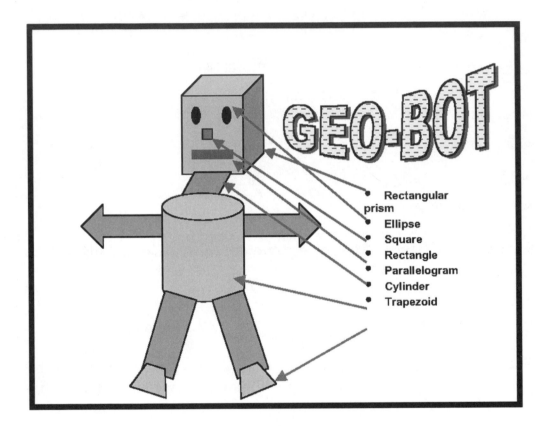

1. Go to View and choose Toolbars, then Drawing. You will use AutoShapes to create a Geo-Bot.

2. Click on AutoShapes and choose Basic Shapes.

3. Choose a shape that you would like to use in your Geo-Bot.

4. Click inside the screen.

5. Move the shape to its position on the Geo-Bot.

6. To rotate or turn the shape, choose the Select Object and Free Rotate buttons located on the Drawing toolbar.

*(continued)*

7. Turn the green circles on the selected shape until you have the shape positioned.

8. Continue to choose shapes and position them on your Geo-Bot. You may make the selected shape larger or smaller by stretching and skewing it.

9. Select the shape to color.

10. Choose the Fill Color button on the Drawing Toolbar and the color you want for the selected shape.

11. Choose WordArt on the Drawing toolbar and choose a style.

12. Type "Geo-Bot" in the message box and choose OK.

13. Use the field handles to size the WordArt.

14. Go to Insert on the menu bar and choose Text Box.

15. Click inside the screen.

16. Choose the Bullet button on the Formatting toolbar. (You may have to format the bullets by choosing Format on the menu bar, Bullets and Numbering, and choosing the bullets in the message box.)

17. Type a list of shapes used in your Geo-Bot. (Hint: Look back in the Basic Shapes section of AutoShapes if you're not sure of the shape's name.)

18. Click on the Arrow button on the Drawing toolbar. Click and drag from the shape name to the shape to insert the arrow. Use the field handles to move and stretch and skew arrows as necessary. You may choose the Arrow Style, Line Style, and Line Color buttons on the Drawing toolbar to format the arrows. (Select the arrows to make changes.)

# Ice Cube

· · · · · · · · · · · · · · · · · · · ◆ · · · · · · · · · · · · · · · · · ·

*Objective:* To identify, draw, and analyze attributes of a cube using the Paint Tool Box and Color Box

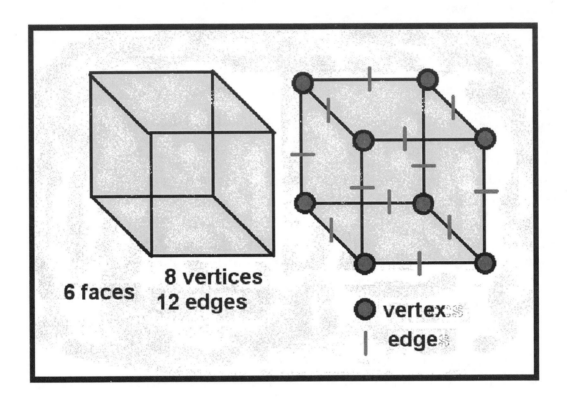

**6 faces**   **8 vertices**
**12 edges**

● **vertex**
│ **edge**

- A *cube* is a regular solid that has six square faces and twelve edges that all have the same length.

**1.** Click on the Line button and choose the third line size from the section at the bottom of the Tool Box.

**2.** Click on the Rectangle button and choose transparent from the section at the bottom of the Tool Box. Drag (while holding down the Shift key) a medium-size square.

**3.** Click on the Select button and choose transparent from the section at the bottom of the Tool Box. Select the square.

*(continued)*

**4.** Go to Edit and choose Copy.

**5.** Go to Edit and choose Paste.

**6.** Click on the Line button and choose red from the Color Box. Make a red dot in the center of the first square using a quick left click.

**7.** Click on the Select button and select the pasted square. Move the pasted square so that the vertex of the upper left angle is on the red dot.

**8.** Click on the Line button and choose black from the Color Box. Drag lines to connect the corners of the squares to form a cube.

**9.** Click on the Fill With Color button and choose light blue from the Color Box. Click in the cube to color it light blue.

**10.** Click on the Airbrush button and make white frost by clicking on the ice cube.

**11.** Click on the Text button and drag a text box to describe the properties of a cube. (How many vertices, edges, and faces does it have?)

**12.** You may mark the edges and vertices using lines or dots as you count.

# Rectangular Prism

*Objective:* To identify, draw, and analyze attributes of a rectangular prism using the Paint Tool Box and Color Box

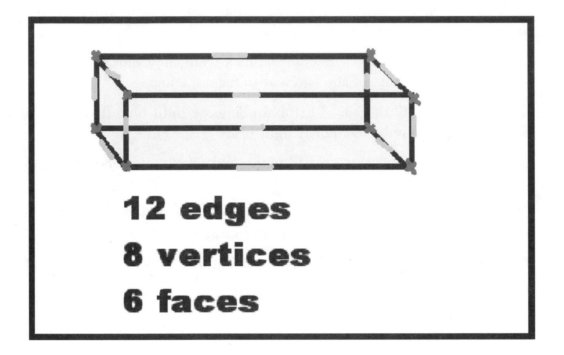

- A *polygon* is a closed plane shape made with straight lines.

- A *polyhedron* is a solid shape that has flat sides. The flat sides, called *faces*, are all polygons.

- A *prism* is a polyhedron with the same shape along its length.

- The *vertices* of a polyhedron are the points where the sides meet.

- A *rectangular prism* is a prism with a rectangular shape at its base.

**1.** Click on the Line button and choose the third line size from the section at the bottom of the Tool Box.

*(continued)*

2. Click on the Rectangle button and choose transparent from the section at the bottom of the Tool Box. Drag a rectangle.

3. Click on the Select button and choose transparent from the section at the bottom of the Tool Box. Select the rectangle.

4. Go to Edit and choose Copy.

5. Go to Edit and choose Paste.

6. Move the pasted rectangle about a half inch below the original's top line and about a half inch to the right.

7. Click on the Line button and drag four lines to connect the corners and make a box. This shape is called a rectangular prism.

8. Click on the Fill With Color button and choose any color from the Color Box. Click inside your box to color it.

9. Click on the Text button and drag a text box. List the properties of a rectangular prism. You may want to click on the Line button and use a different color to mark the vertices and edges.

10. Compare the properties of a cube (see the previous activity) and the properties of a rectangular prism.

# Cylinder

◆

*Objective:* To identify, draw and analyze attributes of a cylinder using the Paint Tool Box and Color Box

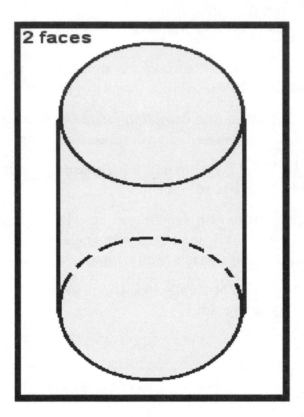

2 faces

- A *cylinder* is a solid shape that has two parallel bases that are congruent circles.

1. Click on the Line button and choose the third line size from the section at the bottom of the Tool Box.

2. Click on the Ellipse button and drag (while holding down the Shift key) a medium-size circle.

3. Click on the Select button and choose transparent from the section at the bottom of the Tool Box. Select the circle.

*(continued)*

· 184 ·

**4.** Go to Edit and choose Copy.

**5.** Go to Edit and choose Paste.

**6.** Move the pasted circle straight above the original circle with a little space in between.

**7.** Click on the Line button and drag lines to connect the two circles on each side.

**8.** Click on the Eraser button and erase parts of the back section of the base (make short clicks) to make a dotted line. This is a drawing of a cylinder.

**9.** Click on the Text button to type the properties of a cylinder (two faces).

# Pyramids

◆

*Objective:* To identify, draw, and analyze attributes of pyramids using the Paint Tool Box and Color Box

- A *pyramid* is a polyhedron with a polygon for a base face and all other faces meeting at one vertex called the apex.

- The *apex* of a pyramid is the point where the sides meet.

1. Click on the Rectangle button and drag a rectangle.

2. Click on the Line button and make a dot (quick click) above the rectangle even with the midpoint of the rectangle's length. The dot will be the apex of the pyramid.

3. Drag a line from the apex to each vertex of your polygon. Use the Eraser button to create the dashed lines on the edges that you would not see if this were an opaque solid.

4. Click on the Line button and draw a triangle.

5. Make a dot above the top of the triangle (the apex).

*(continued)*

**6.** Drag a line from the apex to each vertex of your polygon.

**7.** Click on the curve button and drag to make palm trees. Color the trees and use the Airbrush button to make sand. How many faces, edges, and vertices does the triangle-based pyramid have? How many faces, edges, and vertices does the rectangle-based pyramid have?

**8.** Create other pyramids with bases that are different polygons. How many faces, edges, and vertices do the new pyramids have? Do you see a pattern?

# Cones and Spheres

◆

*Objective:* To identify, draw, and analyze attributes of cones and spheres using the Paint Tool Box and Color Box

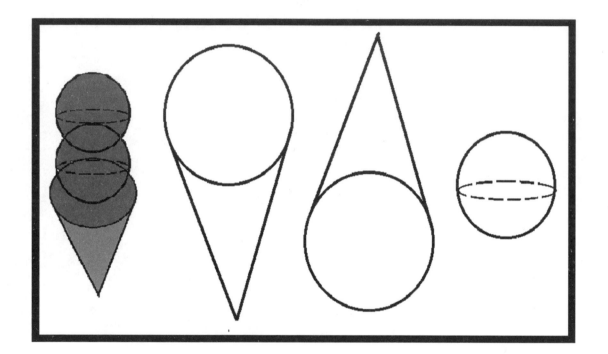

- A *cone* is a solid that has a circular base and narrows to a point at the top, called its vertex.

- A *sphere* is a perfectly round three-dimensional shape.

1. Click on the Line button and choose the third line size from the section at the bottom of the Tool Box.

2. Click on the Ellipse button and choose transparent from the section at the bottom of the Tool Box. Drag (while holding down the Shift key) a medium-size circle.

3. Click on the Line button and make a dot (vertex) midway below the circle.

*(continued)*

4. Use the Line button to drag a line down from each side of the circle to the vertex as in a V. This solid shape is called a cone.

5. Click on the Select button and choose transparent from the section at the bottom of the Tool Box. Select the cone.

6. Go to Edit and choose Copy.

7. Go to Edit and choose Paste.

8. With the pasted cone still selected, go to Images and choose Flip/Rotate, Flip Vertical. This is a flip of the original cone.

9. Click on the Ellipse button and choose transparent from the section at the bottom of the Tool Box. Drag another circle.

10. Drag an oval across the middle of the circle.

11. Click on the Eraser button and choose the second smallest size from the section at the bottom of the Tool Box.

12. Make quick clicks on the oval inside the circle to make a dotted line. This solid shape is called a sphere.

13. Make a smaller cone and sphere.

14. Click on the Select button, select the smaller sphere and move it on top of the smaller cone.

15. Click on the Fill With Color button to make your favorite ice cream cone.

16. Click on the Text button and drag a text box. Type the properties of a cone and a sphere.

# Netting a Cube

◆ ● ● ● ● ● ● ● ● ● ● ● ● ● ● ● ● ● ● ● ◆ ● ● ● ● ● ● ● ● ● ● ● ● ● ● ● ● ● ● ● ◆

*Objective:* To identify and build a three-dimensional object from a two-dimensional representation of that object using the Paint Tool Box and Color Box

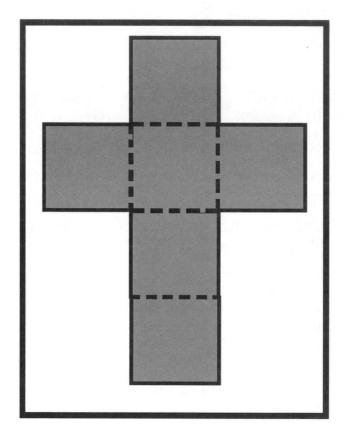

- The *net* of a solid is the two-dimensional shape that can be folded when cut out to form the solid shape.

1. Use an object with a cube shape to study its properties. How many faces does a cube have? Imagine the cube being cut on the edges so that it lies flat. This is the net of a cube. (See the illustration above.)

*(continued)*

2. Click on the Line button and choose the thickest line size from the section at the bottom of the Tool Box.

3. Click on the Rectangle button and choose transparent from the section at the bottom of the Tool Box. Drag (while holding down the Shift button) a medium-size square on the screen.

4. Click on the Select button and choose transparent from the section at the bottom of the Tool Box. Select the square.

5. Go to Edit and choose Copy.

6. Go to Edit and choose Paste.

7. Move the pasted square to connect to the original as you imagined.

8. Continue to paste and move squares until there are six on the net.

9. Click on the Eraser button and click to make a dotted line on the lines to be folded.

10. Click on the Fill With Color button and choose a color from the Color Box to color the net.

11. Go to File and choose Print.

12. Cut out the net and fold along the dotted lines.

13. Tape it lightly with transparent tape.

14. Try netting a rectangular prism.

15. Work with a partner to try to net a square-based pyramid.

# Reflection

◆

*Objective:* To analyze the effect of reflections on geometric figures using the Microsoft Word Drawing toolbar and the Paint Tool Box and Color Box

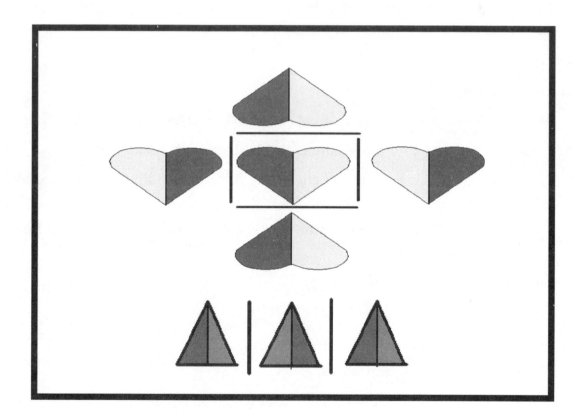

- When you flip a figure over an imaginary line, you make a *reflection*.

1. In Microsoft Word, go to View and choose Toolbars, Drawing, AutoShapes, Basic Shapes. Click on the heart shape.

2. Left click on the screen and adjust the size of the heart to be about an inch in height. (Place the pointer on the left field handle. When the double arrow appears, adjust the size.)

3. Select the heart shape.

*(continued)*

4. Go to Edit and choose Copy.

5. Open Paint.

6. On the Paint window, go to Edit and choose Paste.

7. Move the pasted heart to the center of the screen.

8. Click on the Line button and drag a line of symmetry on the heart.

9. Click on the Fill With Color button to color the left side of the heart red and the right side yellow.

10. Click on the Select button to select the colored heart.

11. Go to Edit and choose Copy.

12. Click on the Line button and choose the thickest line size from the section at the bottom of the Tool Box. Drag lines above, below, and on each side of the heart.

13. Go to Edit and choose Paste.

14. Move the pasted heart above the line over the original heart.

15. Continue to paste and move the pasted hearts until there are four hearts: one above, one below, and one to each side of the lines around the original heart.

16. Click on the Select button and select the top heart.

17. Go to Image and choose Flip/Rotate, Vertical Flip.

18. Select the bottom heart.

19. Go to Image and choose Flip/Rotate, Vertical Flip.

20. Select the side hearts and choose Flip/Rotate, Horizontal Flip.

21. Study your flips. What changes do you see from the original position (the position of the heart in the center)?

22. Click on the Line button and drag three lines to draw a small triangle. Drag a line of symmetry down the middle of the triangle.

23. Click on the Select button and select the triangle. Copy and paste two triangles and place one triangle on each side of the original.

*(continued)*

**24.** Click on the Fill With Color button and choose two colors to color each half of the three triangles in the same way (the right half one color and the left half the other color).

**25.** Click on the Line button and drag a line between the triangles.

**26.** Click on the Select button and use Image, Flip/Rotate to do horizontal flips (reflections) of the triangles.

**27.** Try copying and pasting a triangle with a line of symmetry and using the spray can to color its flip, instead of choosing Flip/Rotate.

**28.** Click on the Text button and drag a text box. Choose Bold, Arial font, size 28, and Underline from the Text toolbar. Type "Reflection or Flip."

# Transformations

◆

*Objective:* To predict and describe the results of sliding, flipping, and turning two-dimensional shapes using the Microsoft Word Drawing toolbar and the Paint Tool Box and Color Box

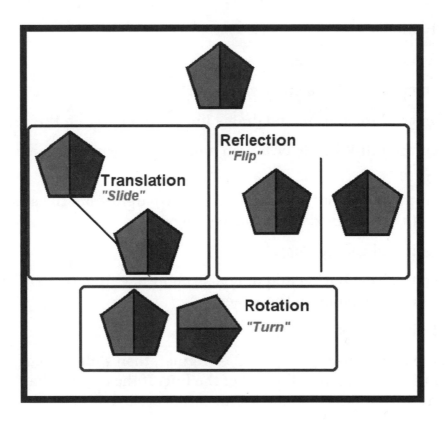

- A *transformation* is the relationship between any original point and its image point.

- A *translation* of a figure is a slide of the figure along a straight line.

- A *rotation* of a figure is a turn of the figure around a point.

- A *reflection* of a figure is a flip of the figure over a line.

1. In Microsoft Word, go to View, Toolbars, and Drawing.

*(continued)*

**2.** On the Drawing toolbar, choose AutoShapes, Basic Shapes, and the Regular Pentagon button.

**3.** Left click inside the screen.

**4.** On the Drawing toolbar, choose the Line Style button and the $1\frac{1}{2}$ pt. line.

**5.** With the pentagon selected, go to Edit and choose Copy.

**6.** Open Paint.

**7.** Go to Edit and choose Paste.

**8.** Move the pasted pentagon down the screen.

**9.** Click on the Line button and drag a line of symmetry on the pentagon.

**10.** Click on the Fill With Color button and color the congruent parts in different colors.

**11.** Click on the Select button and choose transparent from the section at the bottom of the Tool Box. Select the pentagon.

**12.** Go to Edit and choose Copy.

**13.** Click on the Line button and drag a straight line from the bottom of the pentagon to any point on the screen.

**14.** Go to Edit and choose Paste.

**15.** Move the pasted pentagon over the original, then slide it along the straight line and stop at the end of the line. If the original had moved this way, it would have made a translation or slide.

**16.** Go to Edit and choose Paste.

**17.** Move the pasted figure down on the screen.

**18.** Click on the Line button and drag a vertical line to the right of the figure.

**19.** Go to Edit and choose Paste.

**20.** Move the pasted figure to the right of the line.

**21.** Go to Image and choose Flip/Rotate, Flip Horizontal. This shows a reflection, or flip, of the original figure.

**22.** Go to Edit and choose Paste two more times.

*(continued)*

23. Click on Select and select one of the figures.

24. Go to Image and choose Flip/Rotate, Rotate by angle 90°. This shows a rotation, or turn, of the original figure. Notice the position of the colors in each of the transformations.

25. Click on the Text button and drag text boxes to type the name of each transformation.

26. Work with a partner to transform different figures. (One person will do a transformation and the other person will name the type of transformation.)

27. Show your partner a figure.

28. Have your partner turn away from the computer.

29. Make a transformation of the figure.

30. Ask your partner to name the transformation.

# Tessellations

◆

*Objective:* To develop an understanding of tessellation and create a tessellating design using the Microsoft Word Drawing toolbar and the Paint Tool Box and Color Box

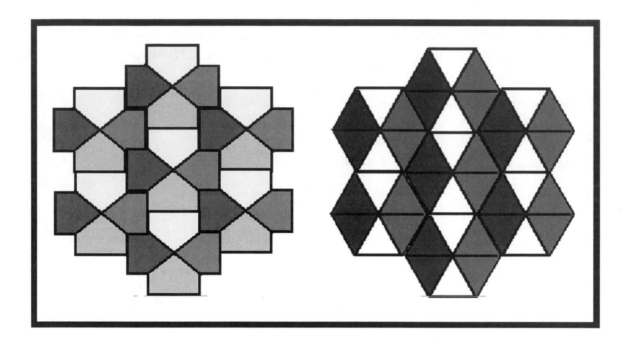

- A *tessellation* is a tiling made by repeating a shape or shapes that completely fill a plane without any gaps or overlaps.

1. In Microsoft Word, go to View and choose Toolbars, Drawing, AutoShapes, Basic Shapes, and the cross.

2. Click inside the screen to insert the cross.

3. Click on the Line Style button on the Drawing toolbar to choose the weight of the line.

4. Go to AutoShapes, Basic Shapes, and Hexagon.

5. Click inside the screen to insert the hexagon.

*(continued)*

6. Select the cross.

7. Go to Edit and choose Copy.

8. Open Paint.

9. Go to Edit and choose Paste.

10. Move the pasted cross to the middle of the screen.

11. Click on the Line button to make a symmetrical design in the cross.

12. Click on the Fill With Color button to color the design.

13. Click on the Select button and choose transparent from the section at the bottom of the Tool Box. Select the cross.

14. Go to Edit and choose Copy.

15. Go to Edit and choose Paste.

16. Move the pasted cross to connect to the original so that the two fit together like a puzzle piece.

17. Continue to paste and connect crosses until the screen is covered. Do you see a pattern? The cross is a shape that can tessellate.

18. Go back to Microsoft Word and copy the octagon.

19. Go back to Paint and paste the octagon.

20. Make a symmetrical design in the octagon.

21. Copy and paste octagons in the same way as the crosses. Does the octagon tessellate?

22. Work with a partner to choose other shapes from Microsoft Word and see if they tessellate.

# Constructing a Triangular Dot Grid

*Objective:* To construct a triangular dot grid to be used for spatial sense and other activities using the Microsoft Word Drawing toolbar and the Paint Tool Box and Color Box

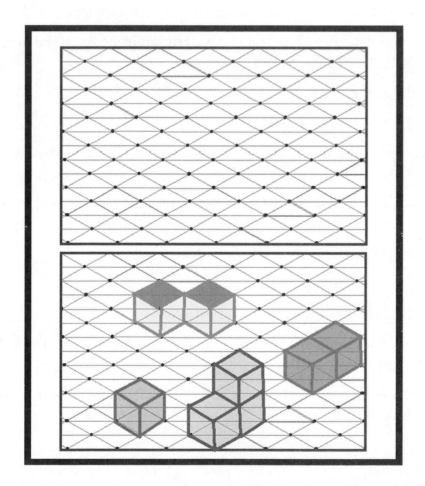

1. In Microsoft Word, go to View and choose Toolbars and Drawing, AutoShapes, Basic Shapes, and Isosceles Triangle.

2. Click on the screen to insert the triangle.

*(continued)*

3. Click on the Line Color button on the Drawing toolbar and choose 40% gray.

4. Select the triangle, go to Edit, and choose Copy.

5. Open Paint.

6. Go to Edit and choose Paste.

7. Click on the Line button and choose the thickest line size from the section at the bottom of the Tool Box.

8. Click on each vertex of the pasted triangle to make a dot.

9. Click on the Select button and choose transparent from the section at the bottom of the Tool Box. Select the triangle.

10. Go to Edit and choose Copy.

11. Choose the Magnifier button in size 2×.

12. Click on the triangle. Now the figure is larger and it will be easier to line up the dots.

13. Go to Edit and choose Paste.

14. Move the pasted triangle so that the lower left dot overlaps the lower right dot of the original.

15. Continue to paste in this way until there are seven triangles.

16. Click on the Select button to select the row of triangles. Move the row to the top of the screen.

17. Go to Edit and choose Copy.

18. Go to Edit and choose Paste.

19. Move the pasted row so that the top vertices overlap the bottom vertices of the original row.

20. Continue to paste rows of triangles in this way.

21. When the screen is full, click on the Magnifier button and choose 1×.

22. When the magnifier is at normal size (1×) and one-quarter of the screen is covered, you may stop.

*(continued)*

**23.** Click on the Rectangle button and choose transparent from the section at the bottom of the Tool Box. Drag a rectangle over the grid to make a medium-size frame.

**24.** Click on the Select button to select and delete lines outside the frame (using the Delete key on the keyboard).

**25.** Choose the Eraser button to erase lines that are close to the frame. (Hint: Use the eraser button with the magnifier for an easy erase.) What patterns do you see in the frame?

**26.** Go to File and choose Save.

**27.** Save with the title "[Your Name]'s Triangular Dot grid."

# Isometric Drawing

*Objective:* To use spatial reasoning to build and draw geometric objects using the Paint Tool Box and Color Box

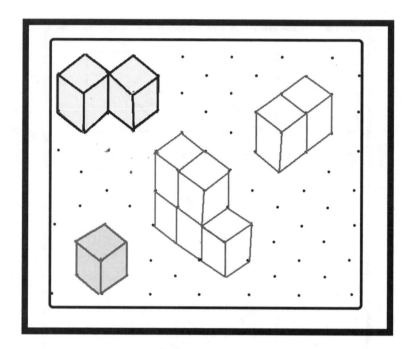

(The teacher should prepare an isometric dot grid in Paint and save it on disks to load into the students' computers.)

1. Open the isometric dot grid prepared by your teacher. The moves on iso-metric dot paper are U (up), D (down), UR (up right), UL (up left), DR (down right), and DL (down left).

2. Click on the Line button and choose a starting dot. Drag lines to move UR1 (up right one), then DR1, D1, DL1, UL1, U1, DR1, D1, U1, and UR1.

3. You have made a cube as viewed from a certain angle.

4. Place a real cube in front of you so that you have about the same view as in your drawing.

5. Try drawing other views of cubes and model the drawings on the dot paper.

# Constructing Tangrams

*Objective:* To construct tangram pieces for use as a math manipulative using the Paint Tool Box and Color Box

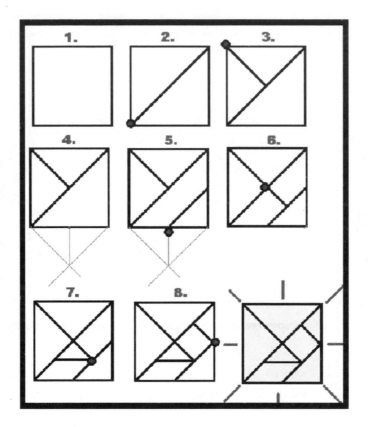

- A *tangram* puzzle is an ancient Chinese puzzle consisting of seven pieces: two large right triangles, one medium right triangle, two small triangles, one square, and one parallelogram.

1. Click on the Line button and choose the fourth line size from the section at the bottom of the Tool Box.

2. Click on the Rectangle button and choose transparent from the section at the bottom of the Tool Box. Drag (while holding down the Shift key) a large square, almost the width of the screen. (See part 1 of the figure.)

*(continued)*

3. Click on the Line button and drag (while holding down the Shift key) a diagonal line from the upper left vertex to the lower right vertex. (See part 2 of the figure.)

4. Drag a line from the upper left vertex until it touches the diagonal line. (See part 3 of the figure.)

5. Choose the thinnest line from the section at the bottom of the Tool Box and light gray from the Color Box.

6. You will bisect (find the midpoint of) the bottom line segment of the square.

7. Place the pointer at the bottom left vertex of the rectangle.

8. Drag (while holding down the Shift key) a 45-degree line going downward to the right. (See part 4 of the figure.)

9. Place the pointer at the right bottom vertex and drag (while holding down the shift key) a 45-degree line going downward to the left as it intersects the other gray line. (See part 4 of the figure.)

10. Place the pointer at the intersection point and drag (while holding down the Shift key) a 90-degree line up to touch the bottom line segment of the rectangle. (See part 4 of the figure.)

11. Choose the thickest line size from the section at the bottom of the Tool Box and red from the Color Box. Click once where the gray line touches the bottom line segment. (See part 4 of the figure.) This red dot is the midpoint of the line segment. Can you explain why?

12. Choose the fourth line size from the section at the bottom of the Tool Box and black from the Color Box.

13. Starting at the midpoint of the base of the rectangle, drag a 45-degree angle line to touch the right side of the square, forming a right triangle. (See part 5 of the figure.)

14. Extend the half diagonal line from Step 3 to touch the line made in Step 5. (See part 6 of the figure.)

15. Starting from the point on the hypotenuse in Step 6, drag a 45-degree line to touch the diagonal line to the right. (See part 7 of the figure.)

*(continued)*

**16.** Starting at the top vertex of the triangle in the lower right corner, drag (while holding down the Shift key) a 90-degree line up to touch the diagonal line. Do you have seven pieces?

**17.** Click on the Fill With Color button to color all the pieces the same color. Which pieces are congruent? What other relationships do you notice?

**18.** Go to File and choose Print.

**19.** Paste the printed tangram square on poster board paper.

**20.** Cut out the square, then cut out the pieces. Your teacher will have many activities for your tangrams.

# Area of Tangram Pieces

*Objective:* To investigate, describe, and analyze the results of subdividing and combining the areas of shapes using the Paint Tool Box and Color Box

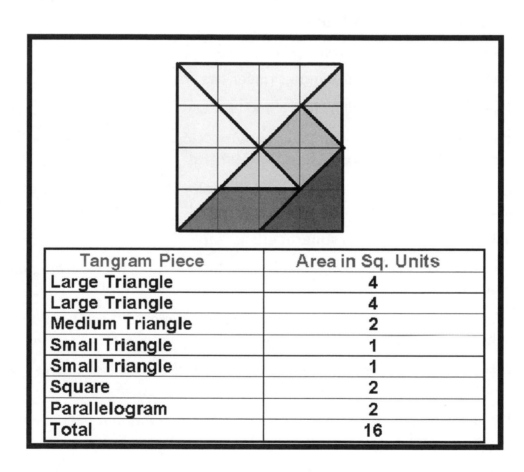

| Tangram Piece | Area in Sq. Units |
|---|---|
| Large Triangle | 4 |
| Large Triangle | 4 |
| Medium Triangle | 2 |
| Small Triangle | 1 |
| Small Triangle | 1 |
| Square | 2 |
| Parallelogram | 2 |
| Total | 16 |

1. Click on the Rectangle button and choose transparent from the section at the bottom of the Tool Box. Drag (while holding down the Shift key) a square.

2. Click on the Select button and choose transparent from the section at the bottom of the Tool Box. Select the square.

3. Go to Edit and choose Copy.

*(continued)*

4. Go to Edit and choose Paste.

5. Move the pasted square to connect to the original (as in a grid).

6. Paste two more squares to make a row of 4 squares.

7. Click on the Select button and select the row of 4 squares.

8. Go to Edit and choose Copy.

9. Go to Edit and choose Paste.

10. Move the pasted row to connect under the original row.

11. Paste two more rows, forming a $4 \times 4$ grid.

12. Follow the steps in the previous activity, "Constructing Tangrams," to make the seven tangram shapes on the grid.

13. Click on the Fill With Color button and color the pairs of congruent pieces the same color and the other pieces different colors.

14. What is the area of the square? (16 sq. units)

15. Use the Rectangle and Line buttons to draw a table for recording data, or use Microsoft Word's Insert Table button to make a table.

16. Calculate the area of each tangram piece and record it on the table. Which pieces have the same area but different shapes?

17. If the area is the same, the perimeter is the same. (Is this a true statement? Can you prove why it is not true?)

18. Work with a partner to calculate and type the fractional part of each piece and prove your calculations.

19. Type any observations and conclusions.

# Constructing a Circular Geoboard

- - - - - - - - - - - - - - - - - - - - - - ◆ - - - - - - - - - - - - - - - - - - - - - -

*Objective:* To construct a circular geoboard using the Paint Tool Box and Color Box

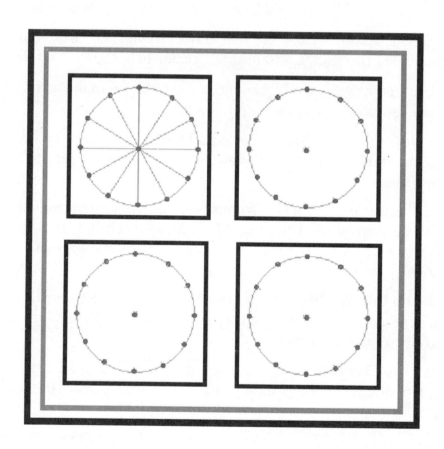

1. Click on the Line button and choose the thinnest line size from the section at the bottom of the Tool Box. Choose light gray from the Color Box.

2. Click on the Ellipse button and choose transparent from the section at the bottom of the Tool Box. Drag (while holding down the Shift key) a circle.

*(continued)*

3. Click on the Line button and drag a line to divide the circle vertically into two equal parts.

4. Drag a line that divides the circle horizontally into two equal parts.

5. Choose the thickest line size from the section at the bottom of the Tool Box and choose red from the Color Box.

6. Place the pointer at the point where the two lines intersect and click to make a red dot. (This should be at about the center of the circle.)

7. Click on the Magnifier button, frame the circle, then click. This will double the size of the image and make it easier to estimate and draw.

8. Click each point where a line touches the circle to make a red dot. Now the circle is divided into four equal parts.

9. Divide each top fourth into three equal parts by making red dots on the edge of the circle. (Remember that if you make a mistake, go to Edit and choose Undo.)

10. Choose the thinnest line size from the section at the bottom of the Tool Box and light gray from the Color Box. Drag a straight line from each new dot through the center of the circle to touch the edge of the other side of the circle.

11. Choose the thickest line size again and red from the Color Box. Make red dots where the lines touch the bottom edge of the circle. The circle is now divided into twelve equal parts.

12. Click on the Eraser button and erase the gray lines inside the circle. (Hint: For erasing close places, position the eraser over the mark and click once.)

13. Click on the Magnifier button again and choose 1×. (This will reduce the figure to normal size.)

14. Click on the Rectangle button and choose transparent from the section at the bottom of the Tool Box. Drag a square frame around the geoboard.

15. Click on the Select button and choose transparent from the section at the bottom of the Tool Box. Select the geoboard and frame.

16. Go to Edit and choose Copy.

*(continued)*

17. Go to Edit and choose Paste.

18. Paste four geoboards.

19. Go to File and choose Save.

20. Save with the title "[Your Name]'s Circular Geoboard."

# Lines in a Circle

· · · · · · · · · · · · · · · · · · · · · ◆ · · · · · · · · · · · · · · · · · · · ·

*Objective:* To draw, recognize, and compare the lines in a circle on a circular geoboard using the Paint Tool Box and Color Box

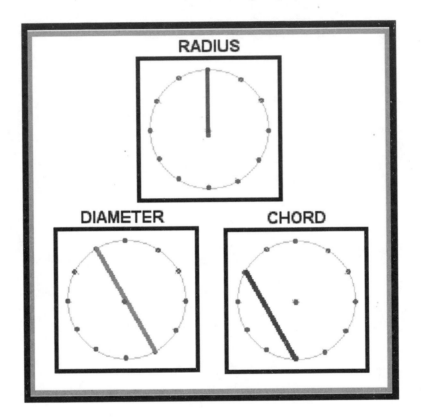

- The *radius* of a circle is the distance from the center of the circle to a point on the circle.

- The *diameter* of a circle is any line that joins two points of the circle and passes through the center.

- A *chord* is a line that joins two points on a circle; if it passes through the center, it is called the diameter.

**1.** Open the document titled "[Your Name]'s Circular Geoboard" that you created in the previous activity.

*(continued)*

2. Click on the Select button and choose transparent from the section at the bottom of the Tool Box. Select a geoboard.

3. Go to Edit and choose Copy.

4. Open Paint.

5. Go to Edit and choose Paste.

6. Move the pasted geoboard down on the screen.

7. Paste two more geoboards.

8. Click on the Line button and choose any color from the Color Box. Draw a radius on one geoboard.

9. Click on the Text button and drag a text box. Type the label "Radius."

10. Draw and label diameter and chord on the other geoboards.

11. Compare radius to diameter. What is the same as half of the diameter?

12. Compare chord to radius. Is the diameter a special kind of chord? If the radius is 3 centimeters, what is the diameter? If the diameter is 12 centimeters, what is the radius?

13. Work with a partner to solve other problems for radius and diameter.

# Section 6

DATA ANALYSIS
AND
PROBABILITY

# Tally

Objective: To develop an understanding of how to tally using the Paint Tool Box

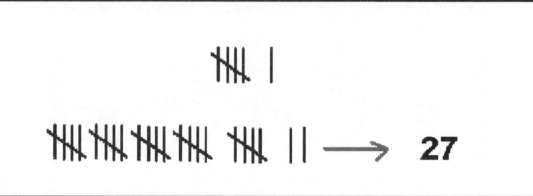

- *Tallies* are marks that represent numbers.

1. Click on the Line button and draw a short, thick line. This tally symbol has a value of one.

2. Click on the Select button and choose transparent from the section at the bottom of the Tool Box. Select the line.

3. Go to Edit and choose Copy.

4. Go to Edit and choose Paste.

5. Move the line next to the original line. This tally shows a value of two.

6. Continue to paste until there are four lines side by side. This tally shows a value of four.

7. Drag a diagonal line across the four lines. This tally shows a value of five.

8. Go to Edit and paste one more line. Position it next to the five tally with extra space in between. This tally shows a value of six.

9. Work with a partner to show tallies for two-digit numbers by copying and pasting the five tally and the one tally.

# Venn Diagram

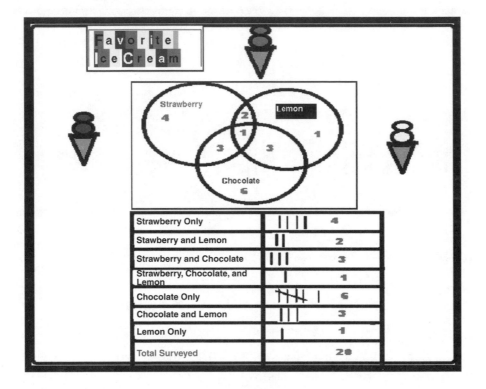

*Objective:* To show how a Venn diagram can be used to organize data containing sets using the Paint Tool Box and Color Box

- A *Venn diagram* is used to show sets. The region inside each circle represents each set, and the universal set is shown by a rectangle.

1. Take a survey on the ice cream flavors your classmates like from the following choices: strawberry, chocolate, and lemon. The data sets will be:

   - Strawberry only

   - Strawberry and Lemon

   - Strawberry and Chocolate

   - Strawberry, Chocolate, and Lemon

*(continued)*

· 218 ·

- Chocolate only

- Chocolate and Lemon

- Lemon only

2. In Paint, click on the Line button and drag lines to draw a two-column table.

3. Click on the Text button and type the name of each set in the first column of the table.

4. Record the results of the survey in the second column of the table. Click on the Line button to make tally marks and click on the Text button to type the numbers for the tallies. From the Text Toolbar, choose Arial font, size 8, and red from the Color Box. Type the words "Strawberry," "Chocolate," and "Lemon" in the color of the flavor.

5. Click on the Ellipse button and choose transparent from the section at the bottom of the Tool Box. Drag a circle.

6. Click on the Select button and select the circle.

7. Go to Edit and choose Copy.

8. Go to Edit and choose Paste.

9. Move the pasted circle to slightly overlap the original.

10. Go to Edit and choose Paste.

11. Move this third circle to slightly overlap both circles.

12. Select and move one flavor name into each circle.

13. Select and copy the totals for each set and move each number to its proper place in the diagram. Remember that the overlaps are for the numbers of people who liked more than one flavor.

# Probability

*Objective:* To develop an understanding of probability using the Paint Tool Box and Color Box

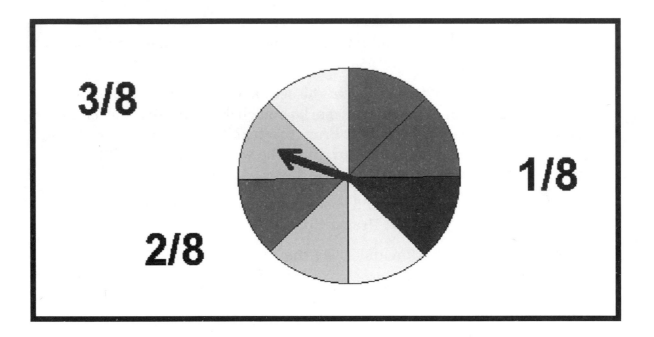

- *Probability* is the measure of how likely an event is to occur.

- The *probability of an event* is a number between 0 and 1.

- Probability is expressed as 4 out of 10, 3 out of 10, and so on.

**1.** Click on the Ellipse button and drag a circle.

**2.** Click on the Line button and drag lines to divide the circle into eight equal parts.

**3.** Click on to Fill With Color button to color one part blue, two parts yellow, two parts green, and three parts red.

**4.** Click on the Line button and choose the thickest line size from the section at the bottom of the Tool Box and brown from the Color Box. Drag lines to form the arrow that will be your spinner.

*(continued)*

**5.** Since there are eight equal parts, the spinner will probably stop on blue one out of eight spins ($\frac{1}{8}$). How many times will the spinner probably stop on red, yellow, and green? ($\frac{3}{8}$, $\frac{2}{8}$, $\frac{2}{8}$)

**6.** Click on the Text button and drag a text box to type the probabilities as fractions. What would be the probability for each color if there were sixteen spins? ($\frac{6}{16}$, $\frac{4}{16}$, $\frac{4}{16}$)

**7.** Click on the Fill With Color button and change the colors on the spinner. What is the probability of the spinner stopping on each color?

**8.** Click on the Text button and drag a text box to type the probabilities as fractions.

**9.** Type your name.

**10.** Go to File and choose Print so that you can exchange papers with your classmates to discuss the probabilities.

# Cube Drawing Probability

*Objective:* To predict the probability of outcomes of simple experiments and test the predictions using the Microsoft Word Drawing toolbar and the Paint Tool Box and Color Box

1. In Microsoft Word, go to View and choose Toolbars, Drawing, AutoShapes, Basic Shapes, and Cube.

2. Click inside the screen to insert the cube.

3. Select the cube.

4. Go to Edit and choose Copy.

5. Open Paint.

6. Go to Edit and choose Paste.

*(continued)*

**7.** Continue to paste until there are ten cubes.

**8.** Click on the Fill With Color button and color four cubes green, three cubes blue, two cubes red, and one cube yellow.

**9.** Click on the Brush or Curve button to draw a bag shape that will hold all the cubes.

**10.** Click on the Select button and choose transparent from the section at the bottom of the Tool Box. Select and move the cubes inside the bag. If you pull a cube from the bag, then return it for a total of ten draws, what is the probability that the cube drawn will be green ($\frac{4}{10}$), blue ($\frac{3}{10}$), red ($\frac{2}{10}$), or yellow ($\frac{1}{10}$)?

**11.** Click on the Text button and type the probability of drawing each color out of ten draws.

**12.** Work with a partner to perform the activity using real colored cubes.

**13.** Keep a tally of the draws. Did your results come close to the probability?

**14.** Click on the Fill With Color button to change the colors and/or paste more cubes and describe the new probabilities.

# Heads or Tails?

◆

*Objective:* To predict the probability of outcomes of simple experiments, test the predictions, and graph the results on a pie chart using the Microsoft Word Formatting toolbar and the Microsoft Excel Chart Wizard

- A *pie chart* is a circular graph divided into sections that shows the contribution of each value to a total value.

1. Choose a partner and predict the number of heads and tails landings for twenty tosses of a penny. What is the percent for each? What was the basis for your prediction?

2. Perform the activity with your partner.

*(continued)*

· 224 ·

3. In Microsoft Word, record the data by typing "H" or "T" for each toss.

4. Total the H's and T's and type the totals.

5. Open Microsoft Excel.

6. Click on the A4 cell and type "Heads."

7. Go to cell A5 by pressing the down arrow key on the keyboard and type "Tails."

8. Click on cell B4 and type the number of times the coin came up heads.

9. Click on cell B5 and type the number of times the coin came up tails.

10. Click on cell A4 and select only the cells that contain data (A4, A5, B4, B5).

11. Choose the Chart Wizard button on the Standard Toolbar.

12. In Step 1, choose the Pie Graph and click on Next.

13. In Step 2, click on Next.

14. In Step 3, title the graph "Penny Toss," and on the Data Labels tab choose Show label and percent. Click on Next.

15. In Step 4, click on Finish. How did your prediction compare with the results? Does the pie graph show about 50% for each?

16. To customize the chart, place the pointer on the area to change and double click, then enter the changes in the message box.

# Bar Graphs

◆

*Objective:* To collect data from an experiment and to represent the data in a bar graph using the Microsoft Excel Chart Wizard.

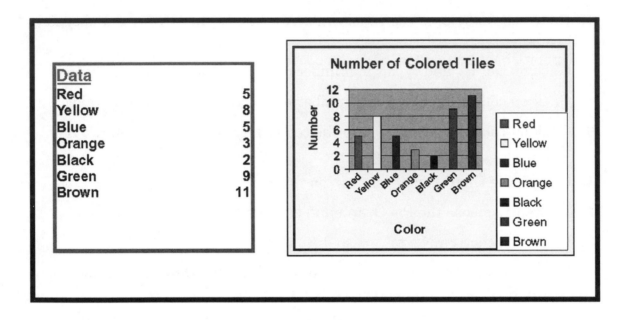

- *Bar graphs* show information in a graphical form by using bars or columns. The height or length of the bar indicates the size of the data it represents.

**1.** Take a handful of colored tiles from a grab bag.

**2.** Sort the tiles by color.

**3.** Open Microsoft Excel, go to File, and choose New.

**4.** In column A, type the names of the colored tiles that you grabbed. (You can move down the column by pressing the down arrow key on the keyboard.)

**5.** In column B, type the number of tiles for each color.

*(continued)*

## Bar Graphs *(continued)*

· · · · · · · · · · · · · · · · · ·

6. Place the pointer on the first cell of your data and hold down the left button on the mouse to select all the cells that contain data.

7. Choose the Chart Wizard button on the Standard Toolbar.

8. In the message box for Step 1, under Standard Types, choose Column and Next.

9. Under Data Range for Step 2, choose Columns and Next.

10. Under Chart Options for Step 3, choose Titles and type "Number of Colored Tiles" for the Chart Title. Click on Next.

11. For Category (*x*) axis, type "Color" and for Category (*y*) axis, type "Number." Click on Next.

12. Under Chart Location for Step 4, choose "As object in." Click on Finish.

13. You may customize your chart by double clicking on the area you want to customize.

14. Change the color of the bars by clicking once on the first bar, then double clicking, choosing the color, and clicking on OK.

15. Double click on the other bars to choose their colors.

16. Go to File and choose Print.

17. Compare your data with those of a classmate. How many tiles did you grab in all? What would be the probability of the different colors that you grabbed?

# Pictographs

· · · · · · · · · · · · · · · ◆ · · · · · · · · · · · · · · ·

*Objective:* To create, compare, and evaluate different representations of the same data using the Microsoft Word Tables and Borders toolbar and the Paint Tool Box and Color Box

| Number of Apples Sold | |
|---|---|
| **Monday** | ꒞꒞꒞꒞ |
| **Tuesday** | ꒞꒞꒞꒞꒞꒞꒞꒞ |
| **Wednesday** | ꒞꒞꒞꒞꒞꒞꒞꒞꒞ |
| **Thursday** | ꒞꒞꒞꒞꒞꒞ |
| **Friday** | ꒞꒞꒞꒞꒞ |

| Number of Apples Sold | |
|---|---|
| **Monday** | 🍎🍎 |
| **Tuesday** | 🍎🍎🍎🍎 |
| **Wednesday** | 🍎🍎🍎🍎◗ |
| **Thursday** | 🍎🍎🍎 |
| **Friday** | 🍎🍎◗ |

Each 🍎 = 10

- A *pictograph* uses a symbol or drawing to represent data.

1. Mrs. Brown's third-grade class sold candy apples. They sold apples from Monday through Friday. Their data table for the number of apples they sold each day is shown above. We will make a pictograph of their data. In Microsoft Word, go to View and choose Toolbars, Tables and Borders.

2. On the Tables and Borders toolbar, choose the Insert Table button.

*(continued)*

# Pictographs *(continued)*

. . . . . . . . . . . . . . . . . . . .

3. In the message box, type 2 for columns and 6 for rows. Click on OK.

4. Select the entire table.

5. On the Formatting toolbar, choose Arial font, size 18.

6. Select the first row.

7. On the Formatting toolbar, choose Arial Black, red color, and Center.

8. On the Tables and Borders toolbar, choose the Split Cells button.

9. In the message box, type 1 for columns. This will make the top row have only one column, where you will type the title for your table: "Number of Apples Sold."

10. Open Paint.

11. Click on the Line button and choose the second line size from the section at the bottom of the Tool Box. Drag (while holding down the Shift key) a small line to use as a tally mark.

12. Click on the Select button and choose transparent from the section at the bottom of the Tool Box. Select the line.

13. Go to Edit and choose Copy.

14. Go to Edit and choose Paste.

15. Move the pasted line next to the original.

16. Continue to paste until there are four close lines in a row.

17. Click on the Line button and drag a diagonal line across the row of lines. This is the tally for the number 5.

18. Click on the Select button and select the tally.

19. Go to Edit and choose Copy.

20. Go back to your Microsoft Word document and place the pointer on the second row in the first column of the table. Type the names of the weekdays down the first column, one in each cell.

21. Place the pointer on the second row in the second column.

22. Go to Edit and choose Paste.

*(continued)*

**23.** Continue to paste until you have tally marks that represent the number of apples sold for each day. Monday: 20, Tuesday: 40, Wednesday: 45, Thursday: 30, Friday: 25. You have completed a table using tally marks for data.

**24.** Place the cursor below the table.

**25.** Choose the Insert Table button again and format the table as before.

**26.** Type "Number of Apples Sold" in the top row.

**27.** Type the days in the first column. (You might want to choose a different color for this.)

**28.** Go back to Paint.

**29.** Left click on black and right click on red in the Color Box.

**30.** Click on the Ellipse button and choose opaque from the section at the bottom of the Tool Box. Drag a small circle for an apple.

**31.** Click on the Line and/or Curve button and choose green from the Color Box. Draw a stem and leaf on the apple.

**32.** Click on the Select button and choose transparent from the section at the bottom of the Tool Box. Select the apple.

**33.** Go to Edit and choose Copy.

**34.** Go to Edit and choose Paste.

**35.** Move the pasted apple down on the screen.

**36.** Click on the Select button and select half of the apple.

**37.** Press the Delete key on the keyboard to make half an apple. Each whole apple will represent 10. Each half apple will represent 5.

**38.** Go back to Microsoft Word and place the cursor in the second column of the Monday row.

**39.** Go to Edit and choose Paste.

**40.** Continue to paste until you have enough apples to represent the number sold for each day. Go back to Paint to copy and paste the half apples.

*(continued)*

**41.** Make a key for the pictograph by typing "Each (and pasting an apple) = 10" at the bottom of the graph.

**42.** Go to File and choose Print.

**43.** Work with a partner to construct questions about the graph for other classmates to answer.

**44.** Discuss the two graphs and describe situations where each could be used.

# Line Graph

· · · · · · · · · · · · · · · · · · · · ◆ · · · · · · · · · · · · · · · · · · · ·

*Objective:* To design an investigation to address a question as an experiment and represent the data on a line graph using the Microsoft Excel Chart Wizard

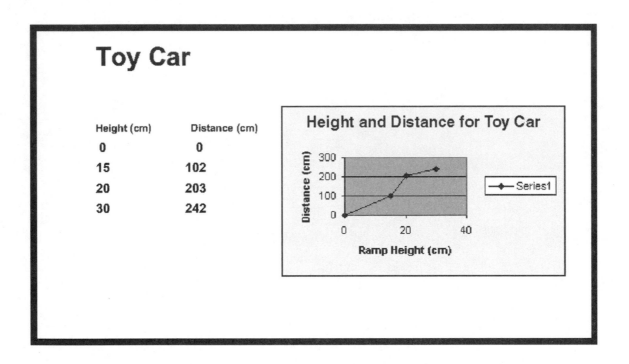

1. If a toy car is released on a ramp, will the height of the ramp affect the stopping distance of the car? To address this question, prepare a ramp that can be set to different heights.

2. To the side of the ramp starting from the base, line several meter sticks end to end.

3. Set the ramp at the lowest height.

4. Place the car at the top of the ramp and release it (do not push).

5. Measure the stopping distance (in centimeters) at the front of the car and record the data.

6. Adjust the ramp for the next height and release the car.

*(continued)*

7. Record the data for at least three heights.

8. Open Microsoft Excel.

9. In cell A4, type 0 for the height.

10. In cell A5, type the first height setting on the ramp.

11. In cell A6, type the second height setting.

12. In cell A7, type the third height setting.

13. In cell B4, type the number 0 for distance.

14. In cells B5, B6, and B7, type the distances the car traveled for each height.

15. Place the pointer on cell A4 and select only the cells containing data.

16. Choose the Chart Wizard button on the Standard Toolbar.

17. In Step 1 under Chart Type, choose Line (with markers displayed at each data value) and click on Next.

18. In Step 2, choose the Series tab and remove the second series, then click on Next.

19. In Step 3 under Chart Title, type "Height and Distance for Toy Car." Under Category (*x*) axis, type "Ramp Height (cm)." Under Category (*y*) axis, type "Distance (cm)." Click on Next.

20. In Step 4, click on Finish.

21. You may customize the graph by double clicking on the area to be changed.

22. Go to File and choose Print.

23. Analyze the graph. Does the distance increase as the height increases? Is the line almost straight? Why?

24. Compare your graph with a classmate's graph. Did the size or weight of the cars make a difference in the distance?

25. Open Microsoft Word and type any conclusions from the information shown on the graph.

# Pie Graph

· · · · · · · · · · · · · · · · · · · ◆ · · · · · · · · · · · · · · · · · · ·

*Objective:* To represent data on a pie graph using the Microsoft Excel Chart Wizard

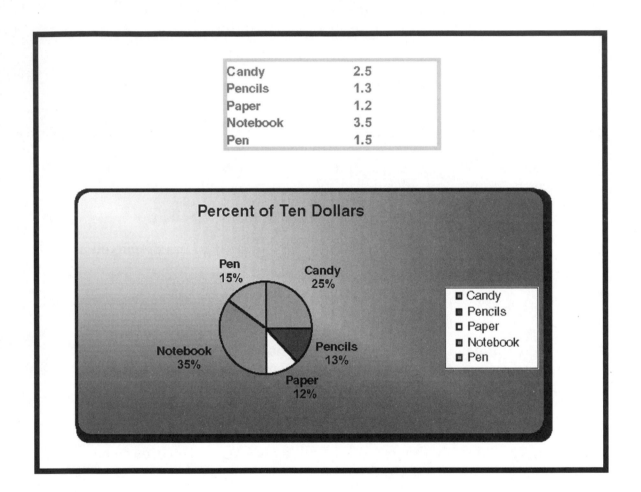

1. Mary had $10.00 to spend. She spent $2.50 on candy, $1.30 on pencils, $1.20 on paper, $3.50 on a notebook, and $1.50 on a pen. Graph the percent of $10.00 spent on each item. In Microsoft Excel, select cell A2 and type the word "Candy."

2. Go to cell A3 and type the word "Pencils."

3. Continue to type the other items in the A column.

*(continued)*

4. Select cell B2 and type the amount (in decimals) spent on candy.

5. Going down the B column, continue to type the amounts spent on each item.

6. Left click on cell A2 and select only the cells that contain data.

7. Choose the Chart Wizard button on the Standard Toolbar.

8. Under Step 1, Chart Type, choose Pie and click on Next.

9. Under Step 2, click on Next.

10. Under Step 3, choose the Title tab and type "Percent of Ten Dollars" under Chart Title.

11. Choose the Data Labels tab and choose Show label and percent. Click on next.

12. Under Step 4, Chart Location, click on Finish.

13. You may customize the graph by double clicking on the graph area.

14. Work with a partner to type questions about the graph.

15. Collect other data and construct another pie graph.

# Mean, Median, Mode, and Range

◆

*Objective:* To develop an understanding of using a data set in determining mean, median, mode, and range using the Microsoft Word Tables and Borders toolbar and the Table Formula functions

| Highest Temperatures for June 23-29 | |
|---|---|
| 90 | June 23 |
| 88 | June 24 |
| 89 | June 25 |
| 87 | June 26 |
| 83 | June 27 |
| 83 | June 28 |
| 86 | June 29 |

| Highest Temperatures for June 23-29 | |
|---|---|
| 83 | June 27 |
| 83 | June 28 |
| 86 | June 29 |
| 87 | June 26 |
| 88 | June 24 |
| 89 | June 25 |
| 90 | June 23 |
| 86.57 | Mean (Average) |

Mean - 86.57, Median - 87, Mode - 83, Range - 7

- The *mean* is the same as the average. The mean of a set of numbers is the sum of the numbers divided by the number of items in the set.

- The *median* of a set of numbers is the middle number once the set is arranged in ascending or descending order.

*(continued)*

- The *mode* of a set of numbers is the most frequently occurring number.

- The *range* of a set of numbers is the difference between the highest and lowest values.

1. Record or obtain the temperatures in your area for a seven-day period.

2. In Microsoft Word, go to the Formatting toolbar and choose center align.

3. Go to View and choose Toolbars, Tables and Borders.

4. Click on the Insert Table button.

5. In the message box, type 2 for the number of columns and 8 for the number of rows. Click on OK.

6. Move the cursor to the outside of the upper left corner of the table until a crossbar appears.

7. Left click on the crossbar to select the entire table.

8. On the Formatting toolbar, choose Arial font, bold, size 16.

9. Place the pointer in the first cell and select the first row.

10. On the Tables and Borders toolbar, choose the Split Cells button.

11. In the message box, type 1 for the number of columns.

12. On the Formatting toolbar choose Arial Black, size 16, and blue. Type the title of the table.

13. Place the pointer on the first cell under the title and select the whole first column.

14. On the Formatting toolbar, change the font color to red and center align.

15. Type the temperatures in the first column and the dates in the second column.

16. Place the pointer outside the table at the upper left corner and click to select the entire table.

17. On the Tables and Borders toolbar, choose a Line Style for the table frame, a Line Weight, and red under Border Color. Click on Outside Border.

*(continued)*

**18.** Select the entire table again.

**19.** Go to Edit and choose Copy.

**20.** Place the cursor under the table and click Enter twice.

**21.** Go to Edit and choose Paste.

**22.** Select the entire pasted table.

**23.** Click on the frame and change the color to blue. You will use the blue-bordered table to find the Mean, Median, and Mode of the set of temperatures.

**24.** Select the first column of the blue table.

**25.** On the Tables and Borders toolbar, choose the Sort Ascending or Sort Descending button. Notice the numbers are now in ascending (counting up) or descending (counting down) order.

**26.** Place the cursor at the end of the last row and outside the table.

**27.** Press Enter on the keyboard to make an additional row.

**28.** Type the word "Mean" in the second column of the last row.

**29.** Select the cell to the left of the "Mean" cell.

**30.** Go to Table on the menu bar and choose Formula.

**31.** In the message box, clear the Formula box and type "=."

**32.** Under Paste Functions, choose Average.

**33.** Type A2:A8 inside the parentheses and click on OK. This cell's function is to average the numbers in the first column, cells A2 to A8. (Cell A1 is the heading.) The mean (average) temperature will automatically appear in cell A9 (86.57).

**34.** Find the middle number in the list (the median). If the list has an even number of items, average the two middle numbers to find the median.

**35.** Place the cursor on that cell and select the row.

**36.** On the Tables and Borders toolbar, choose the Shading Color button options to shade the median cells a light color. What number appears most frequently in the list? (83) This is the mode.

*(continued)*

**37.** Find the difference between the lowest and the highest numbers in the list. This is the range.

**38.** You may want to find an appropriate graphic to decorate your tables. Go to View and choose the Drawing toolbar. Click on Insert Clip Art and choose a picture to insert.

**39.** Discuss situations with your classmates where finding the mean, median, mode, and range of data would be relevant.

**40.** Work with a partner to collect other data and find the mean, median, mode, and range.